A LEVEL COUNTRY

Andrew Hunter Blair

ISBN 1 904136 15 X

PREVIOUSLY PUBLISHED
BY THE AUTHOR

Great Ouse Country

Published by John Nickalls Publications,
Oak Farm Bungalow, Sawyers Lane, Suton,
Wymondham, Norfolk NR 18 9SH

Typeset by Ashley Gray and Printed by Geo R Reeve Ltd,
9–11 Town Green, Wymondham, Norfolk NR18 0BD

A LEVEL COUNTRY

Sketches of its Fenland folk and history

Andrew Hunter Blair

To Emma and Edward

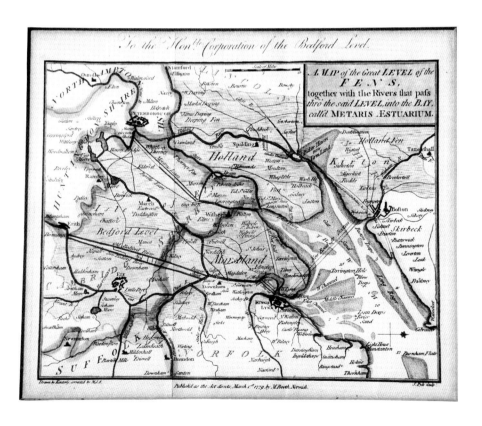

CONTENTS

INDEX OF ILLUSTRATIONS

ACKNOWLEDGEMENTS

Grateful acknowledgement is made to all the authors of the publications listed under Sources, References and Further Reading, which have been used extensively when researching this book. These authors include those who have prepared numerous town, village, church, and conservation guides. The author would also like to thank all those who have given additional information; Anglian Water, The Environment Agency, The Middle Level Commissioners, The Cam Conservancy, The Fens Tourism Group, The Great Ouse Boating Association, Cambridgeshire County Council Libraries and Information Service, Tourist Information Centres, Conservation Bodies, museum staff, as well as those the author met in towns, villages, churches, at marinas, on footpaths, on boats, and at locks and in the country.

The background maps for Chapters 5 to 9 are based on the following Ordnance Survey maps:

Landranger 142, Peterborough, 1:50,000
Landranger 143, Ely & Wisbech, 1:50,000
Landranger 154, Cambridge & Newmarket, 1:50,000

They are reproduced by permission of Ordnance Survey on behalf of the Controller of Her Majesty's Stationery Office, © Crown Copyright MC100036267.

The background map heading Chapter 1 is based on Geological Survey Maps:

Geological Map Sheet 158, Peterborough (S&D) 1984, 1:50,000.
Geological Map Sheet 159, Wisbech (S&D) 1995, 1:50,000.
Geological Map Sheet 172, Ramsey (S&D) 1995, 1:50,000.
Geological Map Sheet 173, Ely (S&D) 1980, 1:50,000.

The author particularly acknowledges the agreement by William Wilson of Imray Laurie Norie and Wilson to the publication of this book which contains some material written previously by the author and published by Imray, and the assistance of Bob Burn-Murdoch of the Norris Library and Museum, St Ives. Special thanks are given to John Nickalls of John Nickalls Publications, Suton, Ashley Gray, and to Geo. R. Reeve Ltd of Wymondham who respectively enabled the publication, design, and printing of this book.

The Old River Nene at Benwick – See Chapter 1

Crowland Abbey – See Chapter 2

Bevill's Leam – See Chapter 3

So flat you can see the curvature of the Earth – See Chapter 4

Lampass Cross, Stanground – See Chapter 5

The Brinks, Wisbech – See Chapter 6

Welche's Dam – See Chapter 7

The New Bedford River at Mepal – See Chapter 8

Reeds drying at Wicken Fen – See Chapter 9

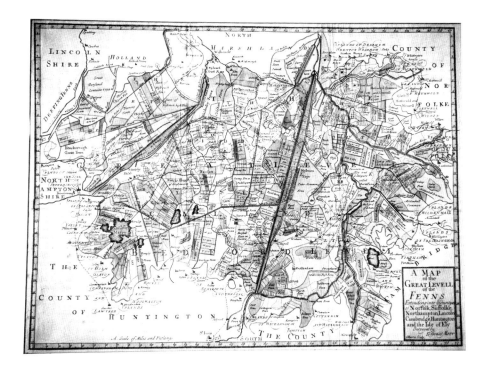

INTRODUCTION

The East Anglian Fenland stretches from Lincoln to Cambridge, 120km, and from Peterborough to Brandon, 58km. It is a flat – level – country comprising generally of ancient silt lands to the north and ancient peat lands to the south. It is this southern part which became known as 'The Great Level of the Fens'. Sir Cornelius Vermuyden, in his Discourse of 1642 (in Summers) describes it as being 'broad and of great extent, and flat, with little or no descent of its own, and grown full of hassocks, sedge and reed; and the rivers full of weeds; and the waters go slowly away from the lands and out of the rivers, and they come swift into and upon it of the Upland Counties where the rivers have a great fall'.

Apart from the fact that the drained land has now become some of the most valuable agricultural land in the country, his description remains remarkably true some 350 years later. Indeed, as over the passage of time East Anglia has sunk and the sea level has risen, the waters, if anything, go even slower away from the lands. Similarly with increased urbanisation and improvements in upland drainage, the waters come even swifter upon it.

The Great Level or Bedford Level was divided into three areas by Vermuyden: from the River Glen to Morton's Leam, from Morton's Leam to the Old Bedford River, and from the Old Bedford River southwards.

The boundary represented by the River Glen was subsequently changed to the River Welland. They became known as The North Level, The Middle Level and The South Level respectively.

A Level Country makes a journey through Fenland from its prehistoric origins through its past and present to its uncertain future. On its way it meets Saints and Devils, Monks and Nuns, Rioters and Rebels, Witches and Werewolves, and Kings and Queens. It passes by magnificent Abbeys and Cathedrals, over a Triangular Bridge and through a Kingdom and a Republic. It finds great engineers, social reformers, writers, poets, and soldiers. It comes across two Whales, a Hippopotamus and a Dog in a Doublet. All have this Level Country in common.

Andrew Hunter Blair is a chartered civil engineer, who was educated at Rugby School and Queen's University, Belfast, where he gained his B.Sc. and M.Sc. Following a short spell with the Great Ouse River Board in Cambridge, he worked for nine years at the Water Research Association/Centre at Medmenham near Henley on Thames, where he pioneered work on the quality and quantity of underground water. During this period he prepared and presented many papers at both national and international conferences. Returning to East Anglia in 1974, he joined Anglian Water headquarters where he worked on the fluvial and tidal aspects of water management. On its formation, he continued this work within the National Rivers Authority at its Anglian Region headquarters in Peterborough. He retired from his post as Regional Co-ordinator in December 1993 after which he undertook consultancy work for Sir William Halcrow and Partners and the Middle Level Commissioners.

Having spent most of his working life in East Anglia, he has grown to know its rivers, particularly the River Great Ouse and those in the Fens. This knowledge has been demonstrated in two practical publications popular with all river users, particularly navigators: *The River Great Ouse and its Tributaries*; a guide for river users and *The Middle Level*; a map and commentary on the Fenland Waterways, both published in 2000 by Imray Laurie Norie and Wilson of St Ives in Cambridgeshire.

As the River Great Ouse flows through this Level Country, so *A level Country* is a companion volume to the popular *Great Ouse Country* (A Hunter Blair, John Nickalls Publications, 2002).

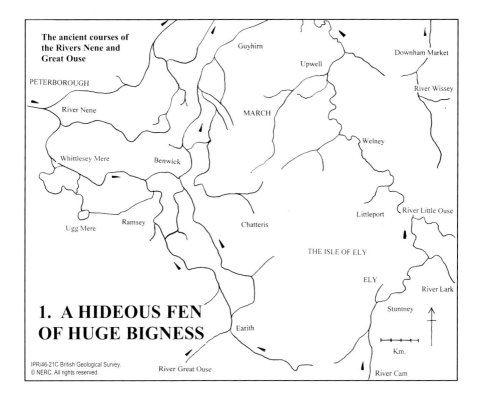

The ancient courses of
the Rivers Nene and
Great Ouse

Guyhirn
Downham Market

Upwell

PETERBOROUGH

River Wissey

River Nene

MARCH

Welney

Whittlesey Mere
Benwick

Littleport
River Little Ouse

Ramsey
Chatteris

Ugg Mere

THE ISLE OF ELY

ELY
River Lark

Stuntney

1. A HIDEOUS FEN
OF HUGE BIGNESS

Earith

Km.

River Great Ouse
River Cam

'There is in Britain a fen of immense size, which begins from the River Grante not far from the city which is named Granteceaster. There are immense marshes, now a black pool of water, now foul running streams, and also many islands, and reeds, and hillocks, and thickets and with manifold windings wide and long it continues up to the north sea.'

Monk Felix in H. C. Darby.

This was how the East Anglian Fens, a great level tract, the largest plain in Britain, appeared to the eighth century Monk Felix. The River Grante to which he refers is the River Cam, in places still known as the River Granta, and the city of Granteceaster is Cambridge. These fens, part of which, some nine centuries later, were to become known as the Great Level of the Fens, had evolved from a complex series of geological events which had started between 100 and 70 million years ago during the early Cretaceous period.

At that time the North Sea extended across much of Britain and North West Europe and in this vast basin depositions of chalk and clay were laid down on the underlying Jurassic clay. There then followed a series of earth movements that raised these deposits to form an enormous landmass joining East Anglia with Europe. Predecessors of the East Anglian rivers, the River Thames, and the River Rhine flowed east and north across this land. As they

1

did so, they gradually eroded away the chalk to form not only huge river basins, of which the Wash is a remnant, but also to create a slightly undulating landscape with scattered outliers of harder rock. These would later become the Fenland 'islands'.

Relatively recently, about 18,000 years ago during the later part of the Pleistocene period, much of this region was covered with ice. As the weather improved, the ice retreated and the basins emerged again, largely unaltered except for a capping of boulder clay on the 'islands'. Not only did the ice retreat, but it melted. This had two very significant consequences; first the sea level rose by up to 100m and secondly East Anglia began to tilt very slowly downwards. Britain became separated from mainland Europe and the sea flooded part of the East Anglian river basin to form the Wash. The remainder of the basin was poised to evolve into today's Fenland.

There then followed a long period during which there was a succession of events resulting in the alternate deposition of silts and clays of both inland and marine origin. Trees and plants became established; in due course they would become peat. Although the major changes had resulted from the melting of the ice caps, there were to be two further significant events. The first was a marine invasion which occurred between 6,000 and 4,000 years ago. The layers of silt and clay, the Barroway Beds, were deposited. These beds killed the underlying trees and plants so forming the first thick layers of peat. When the sea retreated, plants once again became established and as they decayed another layer of peat, the Nordelph Peat, was formed. The second virtually identical event occurred about 2,000 years ago, when the Terrington Beds were deposited on the plants. These beds resulted in the formation of yet more peat.

There were to be many more similar events, but of lesser magnitude, during which layers of either silt or clay were deposited. Whilst generally East Anglia was sinking, there were occasions when the process reversed. During the sinking periods, clay and marine silts were deposited far inland. When the land was rising, fresh water silts were deposited. Not only did these deposits kill the underlying vegetation which had become established during the intervening dry periods, but the plants themselves, which grew in marshy fresh water lagoons, formed additional layers of peat as they decayed.

Because of these long complicated processes, the boundaries between fresh water and marine clays and silts and peat are complex, with layers of one overlapping layers of another. The marine silts and clays have intruded into the peats in a wedge running south from between Wisbech and Downham Market, and south-east from Thorney round March, to Littleport from whence they intruded even further along the river channels towards Cambridge and Lakenheath.

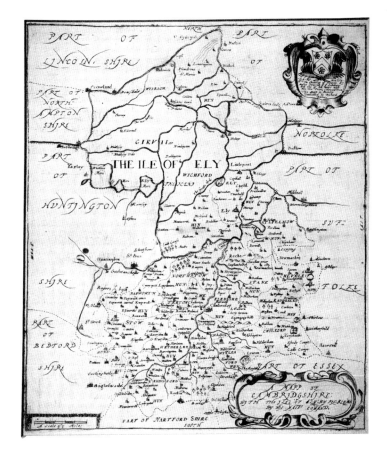

A very complex drainage system of innumerable rivers, streams, meres, lakes, and swamps developed. Whilst it is very difficult to relate this pattern with the major geological events, a general, but complicated, picture emerges which is far removed from that known today. To help understand this pattern latter-day names are used. Three principal rivers entered Fenland; the Nene to the east of Peterborough, the Western Ouse at Earith and the Eastern Ouse near Waterbeach.

The River Nene appears initially to have divided into two main streams. One flowed north-east out of the Middle Level past Flag Fen into the North Level where it appears to have divided again. One branch continued north-east towards St Vincent's Cross near Crowland, along the line of the Cat's Water, before turning east along the course of the Old South Eau towards Clough's Cross. Here it not only rejoined the second branch, which had taken a more direct route through Thorney, but it was also joined with waters from the second main stream of the Nene and indeed from the Western Ouse. It continued north-west to the sea at Tydd St Mary or Wisbech. The second main stream of the Nene initially flowed south-east into the Middle Level

3

where it too divided into two branches. One branch flowed south through Whittlesey Mere towards Benwick, where it was joined by the Western Ouse.

The Western Ouse, the extension of the River Great Ouse, entered Fenland at Earith. After picking up the Old West River, it flowed north for a short distance before dividing into two main streams. The southern stream flowed generally north-west, dividing as it did so. One branch continued north-west in a somewhat erratic manner through Ramsey Mere and then north to join the River Nene to the west of Benwick. The other branch continued north where it was joined by the other main stream of the river which had flowed east, then north and finally north-west from Earith to Benwick.

(See colour section for larger photo)

This large river then flowed north, capturing the second of the two southerly branches of the River Nene which had taken a direct easterly route from Peterborough. Now a major river, it flowed through a delta-like system, north towards Guyhirn and the sea, either directly at Wisbech, or north-west via the longer route to Tydd St Mary.

The Eastern Ouse was the northerly extension of the River Cam. It flowed north, past Stretham towards, but to the east of, Ely, passing close to the higher land at Stuntney. After a series of meanders, it was joined by the predecessor of the River Lark. It then flowed north and then north-west to Littleport where it picked up the predecessor of the River Little Ouse. Flowing past Welney, it was joined by the River Wissey, after which it became united with the River Nene and Western Ouse as they all flowed through a large estuary into the North Sea at Wisbech.

Marlowe gives an alternative version of the formation of the Fens. During the Roman occupation of Britain, the region was governed by the tyrant Valerian. He had a predilection for manhunts and matters came to a head when he captured the beautiful Rowena, daughter of priest Mandru, in order to 'entertain' his guests. Mandru gathered his fellow countrymen and they plotted to overthrow the Romans. Some wanted immediate vengeance; others, including Mandru, wished first to draw up careful plans of attack. During the arguments, the Roman guards appeared and took the seven chief priests prisoner to Valerian's palace where they were tortured. Mandru, having seen his six fellow priests crucified, escaped and went into hiding. Months later a stranger came to the town and warned the British slaves to leave the town that night. Some took his advice and fled; others remained, deriding him. The stranger mysteriously disappeared.

During the night those who had stayed were awoken by a gale. They saw the gates of the town were open and the guards asleep. They escaped and met up with groups who had escaped from other cities. As they were talking, the stranger appeared and revealed himself as Mandru. He led them quickly to the higher neighbouring lands. The gods were angry, the gale increased to a tempest and at mid-day the Romans noticed a cloud moving quickly towards them. This cloud developed into a great wall of water about 100m high which swept inland swallowing up everything including the Romans and their houses. The high land, where the Britons had been, broke the power of the wave, the tempest abated and the water retreated. Where there had been a forest, the land appeared like a vast inland sea with scattered islands. Mandru led his people back to these lands and declared them to be Gyrvii or marsh-men.

As Dougdale (in Russell) pointed out in his History of Imbanking and Draining (1662), God was the first of the Drainers. 'That works Draining are most antient and of divine institution we have testimony of holy scripture: "In the beginning God said 'let the waters be gathered together and let dry land appear' and so it was; And the earth brought forth grass, and herb yielding seed, and the fruit tree yielding fruit after his kind; and God saw that it was good"'.

The first works of any significance in Fenland were those carried out by the Romans, and they included not only flood protection and drainage works, but also roads. Starting on the higher chalk lands to the east of the Fens, a long distance road ran from Swaffham, across the Peddar's Way to enter the Fens near Denver. It then ran west in part on ancient Iron Age trackways and in part on the older silts and clays across the Fens passing Nordelph to a likely Roman fort near Christchurch. It continued past March, Whittlesey, and Stanground to Peterborough. A second more important road, Akeman Street, ran north from Cambridge to Ely, and Littleport, after which it crossed the Little Ouse at Brandon. It then carried on northwards to Southery, Downham and King's Lynn.

Amongst the flood protection and drainage works, the Romans built sea banks and created long waterways by digging channels to connect the existing natural rivers. They carried out these works themselves with, it is said, the assistance of Belgians and not, as would have been the case in the 17th century, the Dutch. Badeslade (in Miller and Skertchley) said that 'The banks which the Romans caused to be raised to guard the low lands of Lincolnshire from the inroads of the ocean, are said to have been the work a colony of foreigners, brought over probably from Belgium, a country of a similar description, the natives of which, from their knowledge and habits, would be eminently fitted for such employment'.

The Roman Sea Banks ran east west along the coast between Wisbech and King's Lynn. At that date both towns lay on the coast and at the start of estuaries. That at Wisbech, where that had been a Roman Camp, was at the junction of the old River Nene and River Ouse, and at the head of a very large estuary. In contrast King's Lynn lay at the head of the tidal estuary of a relatively small river.

The watercourses which the Romans created served a number of functions, principally communication, transport, drainage, and flood protection. They included connecting various natural watercourses, building the Cambridgeshire Lodes and as perhaps their most significant work establishing the Car Dyke. Amongst the works connecting the natural watercourses are those which joined the east and west sections of what is now known in its entirety as the Old West River, joined lengths of the River Great Ouse directly from Ely to Littleport and on to the south of Southery, and joined the Rivers Lark and Little Ouse straight to the Great Ouse.

The Cambridgeshire Lodes, a Lode being the medieval word for a waterway, formed a unique network of waterways joining the villages on the higher eastern edge of Fenland directly to the River Cam. Although some say they were built as boundary markers or as a continuation of highland defences such as the Devil's Dyke, they are generally considered to have been built primarily for transport. At the same time they did convey upland water across the Fens and enabled the Fens themselves to be drained.

By far the most ambitious of the Romans early work however was the building of the Car Dyke. The name Car Dyke simply means a Fen Dyke and indeed some Fens in Lincolnshire are known as Cars to this day. This inland waterway, part natural, part artificial, joined Cambridge with York. Leaving Cambridge, its route was initially along the River Cam to just downstream from Horningsea. Here it left the River Cam and flowed north-west to join the Old West River close to Aldreth. It started to cross the Fens at Earith along watercourses, streams and rivers associated with the old course of the Rivers Great Ouse and Nene, past Benwick to a point west of Peterborough. From Peterborough it continued north through Lincolnshire to join the River Witham and thus connected Cambridge with Lincoln. It was then extended along the Foss Dyke to the Trent and thence via the Yorkshire Ouse to York itself.

There are no contemporary descriptions of Fenland during these very early days. Amongst the earliest descriptions are those of the seventh and eighth century chroniclers. Despite the Roman's efforts of draining and embanking, which were abandoned after their departure by the Saxons, conditions at this date would not be significantly different to those which pertained many years earlier.

On the one hand Fenland 'was a very paradise'. John Leland following his tour through England in 1534–1543, wrote 'The Fens that are now were formerly in the nature of a meadow land, fruitful, healthful, and very profitable to the inhabitants, and yielded much relief to the people of the high countries in the time of drought. From which accounts it sufficiently appears that the most considerable part of the Great Level was antiently sound dry land by nature, well furnished with timber, trees and woods: a great part of which was originally in the nature of forest, and the habitation and shelter of deer, etc., as appears by the horns of these animals having been dug up in the making of drains in several places. That this was the state of the Great Level, when the Romans entered the island, is highly probable'. (in Miller and Skertchley).

It seems likely therefore that when the Romans arrived, they found a countryside with rich grazing and fertile arable fields with turf, sedge, reeds, alders, willows, yew, pine, and vast oak trees 30m to the branches and 4m in girth. The turf and sedge would have been used for firing, the reeds for thatching, and the willows' numerous shoots which grew rapidly after lopping, were formed into a fence to act against the floods. A similar technique, known as 'faggoting' is used to this day The land was interspersed with shallow lakes and meres in and around which there was a copious supply of fish and wildfowl. It was thinly populated by a breed of dark, swarthy, hardy, resourceful Fenlanders who had developed a rude system of embanking. Dio Cassius recorded that they were 'capable of enduring hunger and thirst and hardships of every description... when hiding in the marshes they abide there many days with their heads only out of the water'. (in Summers). Communication was along natural tracks or roads which had formed where silt and gravel layers lay at or near the land surface. Where this was not possible, coracles, made of osier twigs and covered with deer hide, floated across the meres and along the rivers.

The Fens were described by Robert Kingsley as having 'a beauty as of the sea, of boundless expanse and freedom' where 'the bright mere gleemed like a mirror in the mid-day sun'. Whilst in reality it was not quite like this, it had nevertheless a quality and potential which the Romans wished to protect, and develop. For a time, whilst they built their banks and roads, the country prospered. However when they left in the early fifth century, they were followed by the Anglo Saxons who quickly abandoned all the Romans' works.

8

So on the other hand it had become 'A level Fen, a prospect wild and wide' where 'a grave flower scarcely deigned to bloom'. Whilst the Fen was largely uninhabitable, 'excepting in some places which God of purpose raised (as may be thought) to be habitations for his servants who chose to dwell there... (viz. the monks of Ramsey, Thorney and Crowland)'. Amongst the earliest descriptions are those relating to Crowland Abbey, its monks and St Guthlac (663?–714). The land was now 'a hideous fen of huge bigness which beginning at the banks of the River Grante [Cam] extends itself from the south to the north even to the sea' and as for Crowland itself, 'no countryman before that devout servant of Christ, St Guthlac, could endure to dwell in it, by reason that such apparitions of devils were so frequently seen there'. The eighth century Monk Felix of Crowland describes a trackless waste of 'immense marshes.... foule running streams.... oft times clouded with moist and dark vapours'.

The atmosphere was permanently damp and there were often long lasting dense fogs. The air and waters were 'foetid'. Whilst the winters were cold with fierce gales, heavy rain, snow and frequent floods, the summers were hot and dry and the land was plagued with mosquitoes. Its inhabitants were regarded with fear and superstition, albeit they had become, per force, hardy, resourceful and skilled wildfowlers and fishers. Most were racked with rheumatism and suffered from high fevers and ague, a form of malaria and for which relief they had become opium eaters. The shape of their crippled bodies combined with the hallucinatory effects of the opium surely gave rise to some of the more lurid descriptions of the Fens and the Fenlanders.

According to Dugdale (in Wentworth Day), St Guthlac 'discerned his cell to be full of black troops of unclean spirits.... In their looks they were cruel, and of form terrible, having great heads, long necks, lean faces, pale countenances, ill-favoured beards, rough ears, wrinkled foreheads, fierce eyes, stinking mouths, teeth like horses, spitting fire out of their throats, crooked jaws, broad lips, loud voices, burnt hair, great cheeks, high breasts, rugged thighs, bunched knees, bended legs, swollen ancles (sic) preposterous feet, open mouths and hoarse cries'.

There is no doubt a degree of truth in all these descriptions. Whilst Fenland was predominantly a dank, dark, dismal, fog-bound swamp, there were periods when it was bright, dry and productive. Seasons of gloom and marine and fluvial floods were interspersed with sunny, dry and highly prosperous periods.

'Moors, bogs, and weeping fens may learn to smile
And leave in dykes their soon forgotten tears'.

Dyer.

That conditions were somewhat dismal is reflected in the number of Doomsday settlements in Fenland. Whilst there were many settlements around the inland edge and along the coast line, there were no settlements on the peat Fens per se. There were however settlements within the Fens themselves on the silts, such as Benwick, and on the 'islands' such as at Crowland, Thorney, Ramsey, Soham and Ely.

The silt upon which Benwick is built is not the silt that was deposited during the major geological events. Benwick was built on the 'Roddons' or 'Rodhams' of the ancient River Nene and River Great Ouse. These are the rivers' natural embankments or levees. Mirroring the old watercourses, they were formed from the silt deposited each time the rivers overflowed their banks. Made of relatively hard material, they provided foundations for dwellings and roads from Roman times. They form today one of the best means of tracing these long vanished rivers, reflected in sinuous lines of buildings or roads, as light bands of sandy soils contrasting with the dark Fen soil, or as changes in the colour of vegetation.

The 'islands' are the more obvious sites for human habitation and indeed there is evidence of habitation dating from the early Bronze Age. However because of their remote nature and the surrounding 'Fen of immense size', they became attractive to Hermits and Saints. It was inhabited 'yea, much more by devils, as appeareth in the life of St Guthlac, who finding it a place of horror and great solitude, began to inhabit there'.

2. SAINTS AND SINNERS

'Thine eyes shall see the King in his beauty:
they shall behold the land that is very far off.'

Isaiah xxxiii 17

St Guthlac was not the first of the hermits or Saints of the early English Church to establish a religious settlement in, or on the very edge, of this 'far off land', the Fens. That honour probably goes to St Augustine, the first Archbishop of Canterbury, who, accompanied by many monks, had been sent by Pope Gregory in 595 to bring Christianity to Britain. He is said to have built a church, dedicated to the Virgin Mary, in the Isle of Ely at Cratendune about 100 years before St Guthlac, in 597. It was sacked by Penda (577?–655) the heathen King of Mercia from 626 to 655, during his crusade against Christianity. Whilst no traces of this church remain, it seems most likely that Cratendune was just to the west of the present City of Ely. Excavations made in 1999, in connection with a large modern housing development which now covers this ancient site, have provided evidence of a large number of dwellings dating from the Iron Age.

Indeed St Guthlac and his abbey at Crowland were preceded by three other major religious establishments, Soham on the edge of the Fens, and Thorney and Ely on the Fenland Islands.

St Felix (d. 647?), from Burgundy in France, known as 'The Apostle of East Anglia', was consecrated Bishop of East Anglia by Honorius. He established his base at Dunwich in Suffolk and at the western limit of his jurisdiction, founded a monastery at Soham on the site of a former Anglo Saxon pagan cemetery in about 631. It did not last long and was sacked by the Danes in 870. Whilst there are no remains today, it is likely that the parish church of St John, dating from the 12th century was built near or on its site. Indeed a cruciform pagan style brooch dating some half century before St Felix's arrival was discovered in the present churchyard.

Although St Felix is thought to have died in Dunwich, he was initially buried at Soham. However that was not to be his final resting place as some 350 years later during King Canute's reign, his body was moved to Ramsey. This created a friendly rivalry between the two great monasteries of Ramsey and Ely. Boat races were held on Soham Mere between the monks from these foundations, St Felix's bones being the prize.

The first of the great monasteries to be built on a Fenland Isle was Thorney. In 656 Abbot Seaxwulf from the Abbey of *Medeshamstede* (Peterborough) asked Wulfhere, King of Mercia, for a home for some of his anchorite monks. Being by persuasion hermits, they wanted a remote cell and had identified an island which they called Ancarig, Island of the Anchorites. It was here that the abbot wished to build a monastery for them dedicated to St Mary. The King agreed 'O beloved Seaxwulf, thus I approve and grant not only what you desire, but all those things that I know you desire on the Lord's behalf'. (In Anglo Saxon Chronicles).

During its early days, which like Soham were short, it spawned two other foundations. St Tona had a small chapel built at Toneham and in about 699, a Hermit Tatwin took another hermit, Guthlac, by boat to Crowland. Thorney also was sacked by the Danes in 870. However, unlike Soham, it was refounded as a Benedictine abbey 100 years later in 972 by Bishop Ethwold of Winchester and endorsed by King Edgar. It venerated its earlier alliterative anchorite Saints, the martyr Tancred, the confessor Torhtred and his sister Tona and was bequeathed the bodies of local Saints such as Huna of Chatteris, and one half of St Botolph's body. (Apparently the other half went to King Edgar's palace and his head to Ely). The abbey thus became known as 'The Abbey Church of St Mary and St Botolph'.

After the Norman Conquest, which it partially survived, it was reformed. The monks moved back in 1098, by 1109 it had been rebuilt by Abbot Guenther (Gontier or Gunter) of Le Mans and was reconsecrated in 1128. The only approach was by water, generally from Stanground; only boats that held a licence were allowed to visit. This was not the only law made by the monks; they forbade any woman to come within six miles of their precincts.

At about this date, William of Malmesbury wrote of 'a little paradise, as delightful as Heaven itself may be deemed, fen-circled, yet rich in the loftiest trees, where water-meadows delight the eye in rich green, where streamlets glide unchecked through each field. Scarce a spot of ground lies there waste: here are orchids, there vineyards... glorious buildings, whose very size it is a wonder that the ground can support amid such marshes... a vast solitude is here the monk's lot, that they may more closely cling to the things above... if a woman is seen there she is counted a monster, but strangers, if men, are greeted as angels unawares... all is holy silence... from its dense thickets it is called Thorney'. (In Ennion). Its gateway was 'one of the hundred celebrated places' in the 14th century and its abbot sat in the House of Lords.

It was dissolved on 1 December 1539 and with no Bishop to protect it, it was almost completely destroyed, only The Peoples Nave (Abbey Church) surviving on the condition that it became parochial. At that time it had an abbot and 20 monks; its value was listed as only £500-2-5 (equivalent to about £147,600 at February 2002). Part of the remains were given by King Edward VI to John, First Earl of Bedford and he in turn in 1579 gave 40 tons and 146 tons of squared stone (which was shipped via Guyhirn to Cambridge) respectively to Trinity College and for a new chapel at Corpus Christi College in Cambridge. The Abbey Church remained more or less derelict until its restoration, reputedly by Inigo Jones, 1638. Despite this restoration, there remains today an almost melancholy religious calm about the Abbey Church.

It could be argued that Thorney had a close relationship with the major 17th century drainage works carried out by Cornelius Vermuyden on the behest of the Duke of Bedford. Not only had Thorney been a 'pied a terre' of the Earls and Dukes of Bedford since the mid-16th century, but Protestant Huguenots, who had settled at Whittlesey, worshipped at Thorney. In the face of persecution in France, they had left for England and Holland in two waves, the first in 1572 after the St Bartholomew's Day Massacre and the second in 1685 following the revocation of the Edict of Nantes. Whilst Vermuyden may well have influenced the arrival of the Dutch Huguenots, widespread opposition to his drainage works in Yorkshire drove them from their first settlement at Axholme on the Lincolnshire/Yorkshire border to form a colony on the Duke of Bedford's lands near Whittlesey. In 1640 Bishop Wren granted a licence to Stephen de Cursal to preach in French or Latin at the Abbey Church, where the Huguenots had been permitted to hold services.

They were much supported by Oliver Cromwell who in 1654 issued an ordnance. 'If any person of a foreign nation, in league and amity with the Commonwealth, being Protestants, shall become purchasers or farmer of any lands... the said person or persons, their heirs, executors, and administrators, shall be accounted free denizens of this Commonwealth and enjoy the like privileges and advantages for descent to their children, dower to their wives and otherwise as denizens of this Commonwealth ought to enjoy'. (In Rouse).

Five Huguenot pastors are recorded; in 1652, 1674, 1685, 1689 and 1715. A plaque commemorates Ezekiel Danois' death in 1674. 'In unwearied zeal, learning, and strictness of life, he was second to none; a great treasure of literature was here hidden from the world, known to God and himself, few besides'.

It is not surprising that, following the sacking of St Augustine's church, another religious community was founded almost immediately in that 'Queen of the Fenland Isles', the Isle of Ely. In 673 St Etheldreda founded her monastery at Ely. Etheldreda, the daughter of Anna, King of East Anglia, was borne at Exning in 630. After two unsuccessful marriages, first to the 14 year old Prince Tonbert and secondly to Ecgfrid, King of Northumbria, she became a nun and gave all her royal rights, in all about 127 parishes in the Isle of Ely and in Suffolk, to the monastery. She died in 679.

In about 695 her sister Sexburga decided that her body should be moved into the main church. Bede (in Stubbs) describes how having ordered a stone coffin, certain of the brethren went by ship to the 'desolate little city...

Granta cæster, and presently found close to the walls of the city a coffin beautifully wrought of white marble, and covered with a lid also most exactly of the same kind of stone'. It was said that before she died she had had a large tumour or goitre under her jaw. It was lanced and whilst her health appeared to improve, she died three days later. When her body was disinterred prior to being placed in her new coffin, it was found that 'the wound of the incision... healed up, so that in a wonderful manner instead of the open and gaping wound with which she had been buried, there then appeared the slightest traces only of a scar! Besides this, all the linen garments in which the body was wrapped appeared whole, and so new that they seemed to have been put on her chaste limbs that very day'.

In 870 the buildings were sacked by the Danes and it was not until 970 that it was restored by King Edgar as a monastery for Benedictine monks. During the Norman Conquest, the buildings were spared on the condition that the monks and abbots obeyed the King. In 1082 Abbot Simeon started a massive rebuilding programme which, apart from a short interruption during King Stephen's reign, was to continue until about 1345 when the main fabric of the Cathedral was completed. In 1539 it was surrendered to Henry VIII with its Prior and 70 monks and was reorganised as a Dean and Chapter and a grammar school. It suffered under the hand of Oliver Cromwell, who despite being Governor of the Isle of Ely and Champion of the Rights of Fenmen, decapitated all but one of the statues in the Lady Chapel, dismissed the congregation and closed the Cathedral for the next 17 years.

Much remains of the former monastery including that 'Ship of the Fens', the Cathedral, part of the 12th century Monks Infirmary, the 13th century Black Hostelry, the 14th century blood letting house Powchers Hall and the 14th century Porta, the main entrance to the monastery and once used as a prison.

(See colour section for larger photo)

Guthlac, later St Guthlac, was another hermit whose sojourn in the Fens gave birth to a further Fenland abbey, Crowland. Apparently he was the son of Perwald, a Mercian noble, who served in the army, retired and became a monk initially in a monastery at Repton. 'He [Guthlac] came in a boat to one

17

of the solitary desert islands, called Cruland, on St Bartholomew's day, and in a hollow on the side of a heap of turf, built himself a hut in the days of Conrad (Kenred?) King of Mercia'. [Cœnred was King of Mercia from 704 to c718] (in Miller and Skertchley). His landing place might have been at Anchor Church Field, about 1.2km from the Abbey.

He was apparently accompanied by Tatwin from Thorney. How he became acquainted with Tatwin of Thorney is not exactly known. However there was a priest called Tatwine whose parish was at Breedon on the Hill in Derbyshire, just a few kilometres from Repton. So it is quite likely that they knew of each other. Tatwine went on to become Archbishop of Canterbury on 10 June 731. He died in 734 and 'In this year the moon was as if it were suffused with blood'. (in Anglo Saxon Chronicles).

Guthlac had died 20 years earlier in 714 and a year or two after his death, King Æthelbald, who had succeeded King Cœnred and ruled for 41 years, founded a Benedictine abbey on the site of Guthlac's cell. The abbey was sacked by the Danes in 870. It was stripped of its treasures, holy relics, the monks were murdered and the bones of Saints were burnt. The Abbey was rebuilt and, before it was destroyed by fire in 1091, had become wealthy, holding land in 50 parishes through six counties. St Vincent's Cross marks the spot where the estates of Crowland, Thorney and Peterborough met. Interestingly today it is at the meeting place of Lincolnshire, Cambridgeshire and the Soke of Peterborough

It may have had a reputation for frugality:

In Holland in the Fenny Lands
Be sure you mark where Croyland stands.
Croyland wine is but so-so,
Sedge instead of hay doth grow,
A bed like stone wherein to lie
and so begone, without 'good-bye'.

(In Bloom).

At the Dissolution the last abbot was John Welles. He was awarded a handsome pension of £120/year, equivalent to £35,415 at February 2002. The frugal abbey had a value of £1217-5-11, equivalent to about £360,000 at February 2002.

The fourth and last of the early major abbeys of the Great Level was at Ramsey, founded in about 969 on an outcrop pushing into the Fens. According to tradition it was founded as a Benedictine Abbey by Earldorman Ailwyn, foster brother to King Edgar. He was assisted by St Oswald and Monk Abbo from the Benedictine Abbey of Fleury on the Loire. Edward the Confessor exempted it from Episcopal jurisdiction and, well endowed, it was to become the fourth richest foundation in England. Its

lands incorporated Bodsey, at that time a small island just to the north of Ramsey. It continued thus until it was sacked by Geoffrey de Mandeville (Galfrid de Magnaville) in 1143. He expelled the monks and turned it into a garrisoned fortress to hold against King Stephen. He laid much of the Great Level to waste, particularly around Ely. However his reign of terror did not last long and he was killed in 1144 attacking the incomplete Burwell Castle, a castle actually being built on the eastern edge of the Fens by the King as a defence against Geoffrey.

After Geoffrey's death the abbey's fortunes were restored. In 1291, with about 40 monks in residence, it had a revenue of £1,310 per annum, equivalent to about £387,000 at February 2002. It continued to flourish until its dissolution in 1539 when about 30 monks were pensioned off and its annual income was £1,715, about £510,000 at February 2002. At this time, the richest of the Fenland abbeys, it had a value of £1938-15, equivalent to about £572,000 at February 2002.

After the Dissolution many of the buildings were granted to Sir Richard Cromwell, who in turn disposed of much of the fabric. Gonville and Caius College in Cambridge was rebuilt with such fabric and Kings and Trinity Colleges partly rebuilt. Part of the gatehouse was removed to Hinchingbrooke House in Huntingdon. The only remains of the abbey are what is believed to be a 13th century chapel, now built into the Abbey House, which in turn is now part of the Abbey School, and the remains of the gatehouse.

There was a smaller foundation at Chatteris or as it was known at Doomesday, Cetriz. Chatteris and the surrounding area has a long history of habitation. There are a number of barrows and tumuli and Bronze and Iron Age weapons have been found. It is said that St Etheldreda's chaplain, Huna from Ely, lived nearby as a hermit after he had buried St Etheldreda. Honey Farm may be built on the site of his chapel. His body was moved to Thorney after pilgrims experienced cures at his graveside.

Whilst most of medieval Chatteris owed its allegiance to Thorney, a part supported a small convent of Benedictine nuns, founded probably very early in the 11th century (1006–1016) by Aelfwen, wife of King Athelstone and sister of Ednoth, Abbot of Ramsey. (Some suggest however that it was founded earlier, 980, by Aroysia de Clare.) Initially it belonged to Ramsey, but was then annexed to Ely during the reign of Henry 1. Although it was damaged by fire in 1302, in 1347 it housed 15 nuns; at its dissolution there was an abbess, prioress and nine nuns. Other than a few traces of the convent's walls, nothing now remains.

There is a legend of a usurer called Brytstan who lived in Chatteris during the early 12th century. Becoming very ill he vowed that if 'by the divine grace he was restored to health' he would become a monk in St Etheldreda's Benedictine convent at Ely. In due course he recovered and so prepared to keep his vow. However one Robert Malarte, a servant of the King and the Devil, falsely accused Brytstan of wishing to become a monk so that he could conceal his thefts from the King. On the evidence of false witnesses he was convicted in Huntingdon and removed to London where he was imprisoned and tortured. During his sojourn he prayed for deliverance to St Benedict and St Etheldreda to whom he had already committed himself. One night there was a dazzling light in his dungeon and he was aware of two figures, one of which spoke to him. 'I am Etheldreda whom thou hast so ceaselessly invoked and this is St Benedict, in whose habit thou wishest to become a servant of God. Dost thou wish to be free of thy bonds?' St Benedict then took two of the links of his chains, drew them apart and threw them forcefully away. The noise woke the guards who on entering the dungeon found their prisoner free. It was considered a miracle and Brytstan was released from his prison. Rumours of the miracle spread and whilst Queen Matilda wished to keep the chains, Brytstan wanted to take them to Ely; the Queen agreed. He arrived in Ely in due course and took his place as a monk. The chains were hung up in front of the altar. It became a custom to give those pilgrims who came to St Audrey's (Etheldreda) shrine a memento of their visit in the form miniature shackles which later degenerated to ribbons which could be bought amongst the 't'awdry' finery of the annual fairs. (In Stubbs).

There were two much smaller foundations in the Fens, Marmont Priory and Mullicourt Priory. Marmont (or Marmound), founded near Upwell for three Gilbertine cannons in 1204 and annexed to Sempringham in Lincolnshire. It was named after Marmonde on the River Gironde in France. Mullicourt, near Outwell, probably founded in the 10th century for Benedictine Monks, was annexed to Ely. There are no traces of either priory.

Whilst the major religious foundations in the heart of the Fens were of a relatively early date, there were a number of generally more recent foundations around the Fen edge, such as at Peakirk, Denny, Spinney, Commercial End, Isleham, and Wereham.

The Peakirk foundation commemorates St Pega or Pea, sister of St Guthlac, who, it is said, retired to a hermitage there after the death of her brother St Guthlac. It too was sacked by the Danes in 870, reformed only to be destroyed again in 1013. Restored once more, it was made a dependency of Crowland in 1048. The parish church's perpetuation of her name is unique in the country.

Denny was founded in c1160 as a Benedictine cell of Ely for monks driven out of their earlier establishment at Elmeney by frequent flooding. About 20 years later it was handed over by Ely to the Knights Templars who remained there until that order was suppressed in 1308. It was handed over to the Countess of Pembroke who reformed the buildings to receive the Poor Clares c1340–1350, from their small abbey in Waterbeach. Soon after their arrival a certain John de Lexham is said to have broken in and attempted to abduct some of the nuns. The Poor Clares were generally well-to-do Franciscan nuns vowed to poverty and they remained at Denny until the Dissolution. It was a large abbey; in 1379 there were 41 nuns whilst at Ely there were 46 monks. Denny is unique in that it is the only monastic establishment which changed from housing Benedictine monks to housing, via the Knights Templars, Franciscan nuns.

A short distance to the north east is Spinney Abbey. It was founded by Mary de Bassingbourne and Beatrix Malebise (Beatrice Malebiche) in c1215–20 for Augustinian Canons on land that had been owned by the Counts of Brittany since 1086. By 1301 there were seven canons, although for the most part there was only a prior and three canons. According to legend, it was connected by a secret passage to Denny Abbey and its nuns. After Dissolution it fell into private hands and the present stone-built farmhouse incorporates parts of the old abbey. It is said to be haunted: could it be by the prior who was murdered in 1403 by three of his own canons?

Isleham is in the west of the region. A very small, simple Norman chapel is all that remains of the 11th century Benedictine Priory of St Margaret of Antioch. It was built as a cell of the Bretton Abbey of St Jacutus de Insula, according to tradition annexed to Rochester, abandoned by its monks in 1254 and finally dissolved in 1414.

Finally to the north are the sites of the Priory of St Winwaloc near Wereham, and a Premonstratensian house near West Dereham. St Winwaloc was a 5th or 6th century Bretton Saint, founder of the French Abbey of Landevennec. The House near West Dereham was founded by Hubert Walter in 1188. There are few remains of either foundation.

Whilst many of these religious houses would probably initially have been built of wood, as they became established, they became stone built, as indeed did many other of the great religious foundations in East Anglia. Such stone is not indigenous to the Fens, however there was one major source to the west at Barnack. There can be little doubt that the Fenland waterways would have been used to transport such stone and other building materials. Consequently there would have been significant drainage and river improvement works during this period. It is difficult today however to distinguish between such works and those carried out earlier by the Romans.

To a certain extent the Fens languished quietly until drainage works of the 15th century paved the way for the 17th century drainage works which were to change the nature of Fenland for ever.

D E S C R I P T I O N
Des pais inondès, appellés
T H E   F E N N S,
Situés en Angleterre , fur les frontieres des fix
enfuivantes Comtés ou *Shires* , comme Norfolke, Suffolke,
Cambridge With the Ifle of Ely, Huntington,
Northampton & Lincolne.

Es *Fenns* ou pais inondés comme jay dit , font fitués entre ces fufdites fix Comtés & la Mer Septentrionale, au cofté du Levant de l'Angleterre: de London environ cinquante milles Angloifes. Ils ont efté au temps paffé entierement fecqs, & fort bonnes terres, comme il appert par l'hiftoire laiffée par efcrit par un nommé *VVilliam of Malmesbury, qui à vefcu en l'an* 1200. *lequel raconte que ce mefme pais eftoit en fon temps femblable à un vray paradis, car il fembloit eftre un ciel mefme en amiableté & beauté , il portoit auffi fi beaux grands arbres , fi haults troncs , polis & fans aucuns neuds , qu'ils fembloyent attaindre jufques aux eftoilles mefmes. Le pais eftoit tant uni & egual comme la mer , & eftoit chargé avec oultre mefure belle verde herbe, de la venoit que fi quelqu'un fe promenott , il n'avoit à craindre qu'il chopperoit fon pied à quelque genouillet ou haulte place. Il ny avoit pas la moindre piece de terre qui eftoit baffe , laquelle n'apportoit quelque chofe de bon. Tu pourvois icy veoir la terre croiftre avec des pomiers , la encore une fois plantée avec des vignobles, croiffans fi haults , qu'il les failloit eftayer avec des petits baftons.*

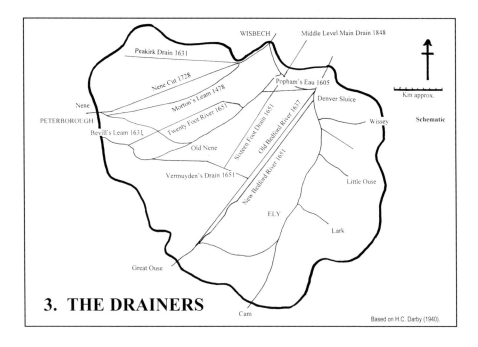

Based on H.C. Darby (1940).

3. THE DRAINERS

Behold the great design, which they do now determine,
Will make our bodies pine, a prey to crows and vermine:
For they do mean all Fens to drain, and waters overmaster,
All will be dry and we must die, 'cause Essex calves want pasture.

Powte's Complaint, 1619.

By the 12th century William of Malmesbury (in Cook) describes a Fenland in which there 'is such plenty of fish as to cause astonishment to strangers, while the natives laugh at their surprise. Waterfowl are as plentiful so that five persons may not only assuage their hunger with both sorts of food, but eat with satiety for a half penny'.

Some saw this potential value of the Fens and carried out the first significant early improvement works since the Romans' embanking and draining works. They were faced with a land covered with meres, swamps and a myriad of all sizes of watercourses surrounding the Fenland Islands. The drainage pattern was so complex that, except for the main rivers, contemporary maps have little in common. The first of the new wave of drainers was John Morton, Bishop of Ely and Lord Chancellor (1420?–1500). He had been elected as Bishop of Ely in 1479 but was probably only in residence there for about four years as he was arrested in 1483 and imprisoned in the Tower of London and Brecknock Castle. After escaping he fled via Ely to Flanders, where he remained until he was summoned to return by Henry VII shortly after which he became

Archbishop of Canterbury. It was perhaps he who first realised that drainage could be best achieved by leading the water across the land in straight channels. To this end he built a direct cut between Stanground near Peterborough and Guyhirn, thus conveying the River Nene along a straight channel some 19km long and 12m wide. To supervise the work he built a tower at Guyhirn from whence he could watch his men. His tower survived until the early 19th century. His channel, Morton's Leam, remains, albeit somewhat modified by successive improvement works over the centuries.

Although Bishop Morton had been the first develop the fundamental technique of relieving flooding and improving drainage by shortening natural meandering watercourses through introducing artificial straight watercourses, it was to be almost 150 years before his principals were further extended by Sir John Popham, Sir Robert Bevill and Sir Cornelius Vermuyden. Fenland as it had been known was set to change for good. No longer would the islands 'be surrounded by bogs and pools, devoid of settled habitation on account of manifold horrors and fears, and the loneliness of the wilde wilderness, so that no man could endure it'. (Bede et al in Summers). An anonymous H. C. (in Darby) had noted that 'the edges of the drowned Fenne being dry, yeelded twice as much grass' as the upland fields. He believed that a drained Fenland would be equally yielding.

(See colour section for larger photo)

Lord Chief Justice Sir John Popham (1531?–1607), a Londoner, invested in drainage works around Upwell in 1605. Although the project was abandoned at his death, some works remain. His legacy is Popham's Eau, a 9km straight cut running from the Old River Nene north-east of March to Well Creek at Nordelph. He established an unpopular principal under which he constructed and maintained drainage works in return for land. Consequently he was hated by poor Fenmen and was described to King James as the 'covetous and bloodie Popham'. This principal was to be used by other drainers with dire consequences.

Both he and Bishop Morton realised that drainage could be improved by leading water away in straight, as opposed to meandering, watercourses. However they had not appreciated that in this flat land, small schemes, whilst they provided local improvement, simply moved the problem elsewhere. The Fens had to be looked at on a regional basis. Sir Robert Bevill recognised these principals and put forward proposals which were later to be adopted by Vermuyden.

There was however a fundamental problem that would face all the future drainers and which remains today. Water needs a slope down which to flow: the steeper the slope the faster the flow; the shallower the slope the slower the flow. However much the drainers straightened the rivers, thus increasing their slope, there remained a limit beyond which they could not go. They could not increase the slope between the western edge of the almost level Fenland and the sea in the east. Vermuyden may have recognised this problem, since amongst his 17th century proposals was a scheme to prevent water crossing Fenland. He proposed digging an artificial river around the eastern edge of the Fens to cut off those rivers that were to cross the Fens. The water which had been cut off was then to be led in another artificial channel directly to the sea. These proposals became reality nearly 300 years after he put them forward.

In the early 17th century, those who wished to drain and exploit the Fens were confronted with the problem of financing such a major undertaking. The solution was to provide those who undertook successful works with various areas of reclaimed land. With this concept in mind, in 1630 Francis 4th Earl of Bedford, who owned land around Thorney and Whittlesey, was asked to drain the whole of southern Fenland in return for 38,500ha (95,000 acres) of land. Of this 16,200ha (40,000 acres) was to be taxed to meet ongoing expenses and 4,900ha (12,000 acres) were to be allocated to the King. The Earl was to receive the balance of 17,400ha (40,000 acres). Under this agreement, the Lynn Law, a concept was adopted which remains to this day as a fundamental plank to the finance of flood protection and land drainage. Those who benefited were to pay an amount such as the Commissioners of Sewers 'judged to be reasonable'. The word 'reasonable' or an interpretation 'fair' still causes problems as there is no strict legal definition for such terms.

In 1631 Francis, and 13 business men, five of whom were from the Fens, formed an association and 'adventured' their capital to provide the necessary funds. Despite objections from the Fenmen, who wanted the Earl to carry out the works, the Dutchman, Sir Cornelius Vermuyden, was appointed as their engineer. It was a strange choice because, to begin with, he was not a drainage engineer. He was formerly a tax inspector in his home town of St Maartensdijk in the province of Zeeland in the Netherlands. In 1621 he was called to England to assist his fellow countryman and land drainage engineer Joachim Liens. His first drainage work, to drain Hatfield Chase in Yorkshire, was not entirely a technical success, and it was a financial disaster for its backers. His works adversely affected a number of commoners and there were riots and loss of life. He was not a popular man. Surprisingly however he was knighted in 1629 and somehow or other his technical reputation was established.

Despite his earlier shortcomings, he was appointed, with terms of reference that were somewhat ambiguous. As he understood it, he was to make summer farming in the Fens reliable and to prevent serious (but not all) winter flooding. Working to the principals of increasing the gradient to the maximum by straightening the meandering rivers and improving sluices and outfalls, he started in 1631. First he built on the Earl's lands, the New South Eau between Crowland and Cloughs Cross (clow being an early word for a sluice) and the Peakirk Drain from Peakirk to Guyhirn. The latter drain, whose course is now reflected in the A47 trunk road, was some 5m wide and 16km long. To the south, he built a cut between Whittlesey Mere and Guyhirn, 12m wide and also 16km long. To the east of the region, he built Sam's Cut, 6m wide and 10km long, from Feltwell in Norfolk to the River Ouse. This continued to drain Methwold Fen naturally until 1883, when soil shrinkage rendered the scheme impractical. During the same period he improved the sluice at Horseshoe on the River Nene at Wisbech.

By far his most important work during this first stage was the building of a new river, the Bedford River, (now the Old Bedford River) 21m wide and 34km long, running in a straight line from a new sluice at Earith to another new sluice at Salter's Lode on the River Great Ouse. It shortened the previous route via Ely and Littleport by about 20km. Initially it was thought that all these works, which had cost about £200,000 (about £17,000,000 at February 2002), were successful and that he had achieved his terms of reference. However within two years this was reversed. The Adventurers only received 16,200ha (40,000 acres) and the King in return for 23,000ha (57,000 acres) also became an Adventurer. Vermuyden received further instructions to achieve year-round farming but before he could put additional works in hand he was interrupted by the Civil War.

After the war in 1649, a new drainage committee was set up. William, the 5th Earl of Bedford (who was to become the 1st Duke of Bedford in 1694), together with the original and new Adventurers, was charged with making the land capable of supporting year-round farming. A year later Vermuyden, despite his unpopularity, was appointed Director of Works. His first move was to divide the Great Level into three administrative areas; the North Level lying between The River Glen and Morton's Leam, the Middle Level lying between Morton's Leam and the Bedford River and the South Level lying to the south and east of the Bedford River. These administrative areas remain roughly as such today.

Once again he embarked on a programme of repairing and completing earlier drainage works, raising banks, building new sluices and cutting new channels. Many of the new channels were named after their width. For example in 1651 he improved the northern part of Bevill's Leam and called it the Twenty Foot River. In the same year the Forty Foot or Vermuyden's Drain lying between Ramsey and Welche's Dam on the (Old) Bedford River and the Sixteen Foot Drain running north-east from the Forty Foot to Popham's Eau were completed. His most important work during this second phase was the building of a new watercourse 34km long running parallel to the (Old) Bedford River, about 1km to the east. Completed in 1651, it became known as the Hundred Foot or New Bedford River. A new sluice was built at Denver to 'hold in and lett goe the water as there bee occasion and preserve the navigation'. Great banks, the Barrier Banks, were built to the west of the Old Bedford River and to the east of the New Bedford River. The land lying between these two rivers, the Great Ouse Washes or Hundred Foot Washes, acted as a vast reservoir, some 2,270ha, in which flood water could be stored before finding its way to the sea. It is said that he employed over 11,000 when building the New Bedford River. Amongst the labourers were Scottish and Dutch prisoners together with a colony of Frenchmen.

The last of his works, Tong's drain which lay outside the Great Level and ran as a relief channel from Nordelph to Well Creek, was completed in 1653. After this it was generally accepted that the aims had been achieved, but at a total cost of some £500,000 (£40,000,000 at February 2002). The original 38,500ha (95,000 acres) of land was finally shared out between the Adventurers and was small recompense to some who had become virtually bankrupt by the venture. Vermuyden's personal involvement with the Fens finished in 1655 and he died in 1677. It was not however the end of his proposed works as his ideas were to be taken up again some 300 years later.

Following the 17th century drainage works, a 19th century geographer (in Astbury) describes Fens in a partly retrospective account. They 'are no longer plagued by winter fogs and summer mosquitoes; and fen ague, a form of malaria which brought about shivering, intense pain in the limbs, fever and violent thirst, is no more. No longer can it be said that Fenmen are a thirsty tribe and avail themselves of the excuse of a moist air and bad water to counteract the former, and correct the latter, by potations of as much strong beer as they can procure: while opium eating and brandy drinking, two palliatives which for a time outlived the complaint, are no longer a drain on the pocket of the fenman or a menace to the health of his children'.

Although most of the drainage works in the Middle Level had been completed by the end of the 17th century, there were to be three further major works in the North and South Levels. First, in the North Level, was an unsuccessful attempt to improve drainage below Wisbech. It was hoped that this could be achieved by straightening, and thus shortening, the natural course of the River Nene between Peterborough and Guyhirn. Hence the River Nene Cut was dug in 1728. Secondly, in the South Level, the old course of the River Great Ouse was also straightened and shortened between Ely and Littleport. This was achieved by the Ouse Cut (1827).

The third and most important of these later works was the final realisation of Vermuyden's original proposals. In 1954 it was proposed that the flow of the rivers Wissey, Lark and Little Ouse be intercepted by a new 'cut-off' channel and led straight to Denver, where a relief channel leading to the sea near King's Lynn was to be built. The works were completed in 1964 and it is noteworthy that they follow almost exactly the route proposed by Vermuyden some 324 years earlier. One can not help wondering at a few prophetic words in Powte's Complaint written in 1619: *'cause Essex calves want pasture.* In the early 1970s modifications were made at Denver to enable water to be diverted from the River Great Ouse into the cut-off from whence it can be abstracted and transferred via pumping stations, pipes and natural and artificial watercourses to reservoirs some 145km distant in South Essex.

It must be mentioned that all these drainage works in the Great Level have been continuously maintained, modified, improved, widened, and rebuilt. Also they were not carried out in isolation. Further works were needed outside the area to lead the newly drained water directly to the sea. Such works included Tong's Drain (1653), the Nene Outfall Cut (1830), Kinderley's Cut (1773), the Eau Brink Cut (1821), the North Level Main Drain (1831) and the Middle Level Main Drain (1848), together with associated sluices, pumps and embankments.

Whether the works were successful depends on various points of view. Vermuyden was unpopular and there were frequent riots, the first being at Holme Fen in 1632. In 1638 there were riots at Whelpmore near Littleport, Coveney, Wicken and Littleport itself and treason and mutiny were threatened. Sir Miles Sandys (in Darby) wrote that if 'order not be taken, it will turn out to be a general rebellion in all the Fen towns'. During Vermuyden's second phase of works, there were further riots and drainage works were destroyed. There were natural and man-made disasters. For example following a great storm in 1713, Denver Sluice collapsed and shortly afterwards, following a riot in 1722, works on the outfall of the River Nene were destroyed and the whole of the North Level remained flooded for a year.

On the other hand his works were judged to have enabled year round farming through out some 16,200ha (40,000 acres). A 'decree of sewers' made in 1653 at Ely declared that the whole of the Great Level was fully drained.

It is doubtful however if these early drainers would have been aware of two further influences. The first was, in part, a long lasting consequence of the Ice Age, namely East Anglia was and is slowly sinking whilst at the same time, the sea level was and is rising. These two factors combine to decrease the slope even more. Secondly in due course they were to become victims of their own success. As the land was drained and exploited, it sank, so much so that much of it was to lie not only below the rivers but also below sea level. This problem was probably recognised by the early 19th century. In c1851, following the drainage of Whittlesey Mere, an iron post, reputedly used at the Great Exhibition, was driven through the peat at Holme Fen. Secured to the top of earlier oak piles which had been driven into the underlying clay, its top was made level with the ground and thus provided a permanent measuring stick. By 1957 the level of the surrounding ground had dropped by about 3.5m. To measure further shrinkage, a second post was installed nearby on a concrete pile driven into the clay. The posts are situated some 45km from the Wash and the land now lies about 3m below sea level implying an annual average lowering of nearly 4cm.

Responsibility for the drainage works, and now perhaps more importantly flood protection works, has passed through a number of hands. Presently it lies with regulatory bodies such as the Environment Agency, Internal Drainage Boards and local authorities, and riparian owners. The modern administrative system is very complicated. The Environment Agency has an over-all supervisory role and is empowered to raise money, make by-laws, carry out works. Amongst other things, it has a national responsibility for strategic rivers, flood defences, flood warning and navigation. The autonomous Internal Drainage Boards have similar powers, but at a more local level. In the Great Level, whilst some, generally larger, Boards operate on an individual basis, others operate under an umbrella organisation, The Middle Level Commissioners. These regulatory bodies have *powers* to do the works; there is an implied, but not regulatory, *duty*.

Works are financed from funds raised nationally and locally, generally on the basis that those who benefit, pay. Under certain circumstances funds move backwards and forwards between the Boards and the Agency. For example where Drainage Boards carry out works which should have been carried out by the Environment Agency, the Agency transfers funds to the Boards. Alternatively, where for example the Boards benefit from the Agency's works, the Boards transfer funds to the Agency. Regardless of who actually carries out the works, they are all subject to a benefit-cost analysis. This has to demonstrate that they will yield a net financial benefit during the life of the particular works.

The administration of land drainage and flood defences which originates from Land Drainage Acts of the early 20th century, is unnecessarily complicated. Large organisations, whilst possibly providing economies of scale, become by definition, remote. They do not always understand the local problems and this is particularly true in the 'rivers' industry where local knowledge has been handed down father to son for years. This was illustrated when 'remote' engineers put on an emergency exercise. Amongst the scenarios that were staged, was one where a large private river cruiser became wedged between lock gates during a serious flood. The organisers had anticipated that those attending the incident would arrange for the vessel to be removed by crane. The only suitable crane was some 80km away, would require a police escort and would take several hours to reach the site. First at the scene of the incident was a foreman who had been heavily involved in the disastrous 1953 floods. Straightaway he said that his gang would immediately smash the boat to pieces and thus clear the lock and enable it to be closed, so preventing serious flooding. He was right; his course of action would have prevented serious flooding causing many thousands of pounds worth of damage. By comparison, the minimal compensation could be sorted out at a later date.

Whilst the drainers shaped Fenland, many of the old rivers have disappeared and the drains now flow in embanked channels high above the surrounding land. The windmills which first raised the water into these high level channels have been replaced in turn by steam in the early 19th century, diesel in the 1920s, and now electric pumps with sophisticated automatic controls. They will have to become larger and more efficient as Fenland continues to be exploited and sinks relative to the sea. The drainage channels will have to be improved to cater for greater river flows from the surrounding higher lands. These arise partly from housing and industrial developments, some of them ill conceived, and partly from more efficient agricultural drainage.

Fenland of the early 21st century is far removed from that which faced the Drainers. It is a land of contrasts; flat and low lying yet interspersed with 'islands', criss-crossed with straight drains, straight railway lines and straight roads which have sudden right-angle bends. It is a land with an immense skyscape whose blue skies with brilliant sunshine contrast with spectacular thunderstorms or winter snowstorms. It can be roasting in the summer when a dry wind can whip away the seeded top soil in 'Fen Blows'. It can be perishing in the winter with bitter north-east winds and frozen dykes; skaters come out on the frozen Washes. It can be dry in the summer and great plumes of irrigation water, taken from the drains, scatter the landscape. It can be wet in the winter with pumps running flat out, dykes running bank full, and the Washes flooded. It is a rich and prosperous land with massive farms providing much of the nation's vegetables. Above all it is a hard worked and hard working land which is now showing some signs of exhaustion as the peat soils waste and wear away to expose the underlying clay.

Despite the drainers' efforts, at the end of the day nature will triumph. Fenland is inexorably moving towards another period of inundation and will return to primeval conditions, ready for a future generation of drainers.

4. A HIPPOPOTAMUS, NO. 7 TOBY AND THE RED ROVER

He spreds his nets alike for pike and eels;
Makes laws at pleasure and then repeals.
In wild seclusion hid he lives afloat
With sprit and gun arranged in open boat.

Dean Duport of Peterborough, 1676.

The local coracles and the Roman vessels were amongst the first to navigate the maze of inland waterways and meres. In the Fens, these were the highways, far more efficient than roads, along which goods and passengers were conveyed. In the early Middle Ages, much trade originated at the port of Wisbech, then at the head of a great coastal estuary. During the 13th century as this estuary became choked with silt and sand, the waters began to flow from Outwell along Well Creek to Wiggenhall and the sea at King's Lynn. Roughly at the same time the eastern part of the River Great Ouse, and with it the River Cam was diverted at Littleport to flow directly towards King's Lynn. By the end of the 14th century Well Creek had become a key link in a water highway between the Midlands and the sea at King's Lynn, to which Cambridge and Ely now had a direct link.

The waterways served local, national and even international needs. They were used to convey people, cloth, wax, tallow, lead and, importantly, building stone from the quarries at Barnack near Peterborough. Merchants from mainland Europe brought in a wide range of goods such as cloth, hides, furs, wool, timber, silk and iron. There were however conflicts and on two occasions, in 1301 and 1331, Well Creek was obstructed. Consequently vessels passing from Peterborough and March to King's Lynn, had to travel down a far longer route, past Welney to Littleport and then back up the Eastern Ouse to King's Lynn. During these times the price of goods increased.

These conflicts between those who wished to use the watercourses to drain the land and those who wished to use them for navigation were to continue to the present day. To attempt to protect the navigators' interests, the Lynn Law was passed in 1630. It provided inter alia that passage along all navigable rivers in the Fens should be preserved. The Bedford Level Corporation, established in 1663, had the conflicting responsibilities for the maintenance of drainage and navigation. As far as navigation was concerned it was placed under a statutory obligation to maintain standards to no lesser degree than the pre-existing standards. It is noteworthy that a similar requirement was incorporated in the Anglian Water Act of 1974.

Despite such disputes and conflicts of interest, river traffic steadily increased. In March 1777, the House of Commons was told the 'between 4 May 1776 and 3 February 1777 as many as 2692 boats and lighters had passed on the Hundred Foot River, and they had been hauled by 1265 pretty large horses'. (In Darby). Such heavy traffic inevitably caused further problems. The vessels damaged the sides of the banks, whilst the horses damaged both the sides and the top.

Before the advent of steam, the vessels were either sailed, or towed by horses. When neither was possible, they were 'quanted'. This consisted of two watermen walking in turns aft along the side of the boat whilst holding a long pole or 'quant' firmly embedded in the river bed, thus pushing the boat forwards.

In 1774, George Walpole, 3rd Earl of Orford, with his mistress Martha Turk and about a dozen other people undertook a voyage around the Fens. George styled himself as Admiral and his 'fleet' comprised of four sail boats, *The Whale, The Alligator, The Shark* and *The Dolphin*. These were accompanied by three tenders, *The Pristis, The Centaurus* and *The Chimera* and two other vessels, a horse-boat and victualler *The Cocoa Nut*, and a 'bumketch' or 'bomb-ketch' *Fireaway*, possibly armed with a heavy Fenland punt gun. The fleet was the forerunner of the traditional 'gang'. This consisted of a 'fore-lighter' in which spare horses were kept, a 'house-lighter' for the crew, a series of decked and open boats for cargo, and finally a small lighter, the 'horse-boat', which was used to move the horses from one side of the river to the other when there was no convenient bridge.

They set off down the River Little Ouse on Sunday, July 17 at twenty past twelve from a point about a 1.5km north west of Lakenheath. The wind was against them and they were towed by a large Fen horse called *The Hippopotamus*. The next day, after passing through Denver Sluice, they entered the Fens at Salter's Lode. They continued down the old course of the River Nene to March and Stanground and arrived in Peterborough on 20 July. After spending several days on Whittlesey Mere, they returned via Ramsey Mere to Lakenheath which they reached on 6 August.

The voyage was conducted in a carnival spirit. It was both entertaining and an entertainment. There were sailing races on Whittlesey Mere where a real Admiral joined the fleet; the 4th Earl of Sandwich, 1st Lord of the Admiralty. There were fishing matches for the copious quantities of eels, perch, and pike. The fleet was an object of curiosity and they were watched with astonishment from the banks by people and animals alike. They in turn made comments, often very derogatory, about the country, the rivers, and the people. The country was flat, simple, fertile and full of 'remarkably fine cattle'. It was 'like some of the best Flemish landscape'. However the old course of the River Nene was 'very narrow, foul, full of weeds and very difficulty navigable'. The houses were clean, but not only were the inhabitants 'meanly clad and dirty', but they also had 'a disagreeable, sallow complexion, broad flat nose and wide mouth predominating'. Whilst the Admiral himself was particularly disparaging about the older women of Upwell, Outwell and March, whom he described as being 'in general extremely ugly', he was taken by the ladies of Ramsey. They were handsome 'with fair hair and good shapes, with expression, and life in their countenances'. (all in Jenkins).

At Denver they noted that a very large bank of sand had formed by the eastern pier. This bank is still a problem for navigators 230 years on. Navigation is currently the responsibility of the Environment Agency and the Middle Level Commissioners. Their laws and by-laws are designed to ensure as far as possible the safety and mutual enjoyment of the rivers by all. The Agency is responsible for the management of navigation on the River Great Ouse and its tributaries, and on the River Nene. The Commissioners are responsible for navigation across the Middle Level between these two rivers. The preferred route starts at Salter's Lode lock on the tidal River Great Ouse below Denver. It goes west along Well Creek, past Nordelph, to Outwell. Here it joins the old course of the River Nene and turns south-west through Upwell and March to Flood's Ferry. Next it turns west again along the Whittlesey Dyke and the King's Dyke to Stanground where it joins the River Nene. Despite a right angled bend at Whittlesey, craft of up to 21m in length can navigate the route.

There is another entrance to the Middle Level. On occasions, it is possible to leave the River Great Ouse at the Old Bedford Sluice and enter the Middle Level via the Old Bedford River at Welche's Dam Lock. This lock is named after the engineer Edmund Welche who worked for Vermuyden. Shortly after Vermuyden's Drain had been built, he had to build a dam in the Old Bedford River to prevent water introduced from the new drain flowing back to Earith. Navigation of this route is however often severely restricted due to heavy siltation at the sluice.

From either route it is possible to navigate to Benwick, Ramsey, Holme Fen and close to Chatteris. It may become possible to navigate direct from Earith to Chatteris and Benwick along a new purpose built waterway. However whilst the initial plans were drawn up in 2003, it is unlikely that such a route would become a reality before 2025.

There is now no commercial navigation in the Middle Level; the arrival of the steam railways in the mid-19th century had signalled its end. Ironically steam boats had just been introduced to the Fenland waterways. Ely had become the centre and in 1824 horse drawn boats were replaced by a 22m steam packet boat. In the late 19th century, steam boats plying the River Great Ouse to King's Lynn, included the 70 tonne cargo boat, the *Nancy* and two tugs the *Annie* and the *Olga.* Steam on rivers could not withstand the onslaught of steam on land.

Although George Stephenson thought, in 1829, that he had mastered the art of building railways across marshes, building railways across the Fens was not simple. On the extreme west of the Great Level, the London to York line crossed the relatively wet Holme Fen. Here the technique was to slowly build up the embankment with alternate layers of faggots and peat sods. As this weight was gradually added, the water was squeezed out of the peat without damaging the fibres. Ballast was then laid on the top; some seven times more than on 'ordinary' lines. On the Cambridge to Ely line, where the soils were better drained, generally only ballast was needed.

As drainage of the fen soils continued, the peat sank, not only due to that drainage, but also due to the increasing weight of the embankments and the rolling stock. This produced changes in gradients, particularly for example up and over the harder rodhams or islands. The tracks could not be allowed to 'hang', and so there had to be a continual programme of maintenance, increasing the ballast. Another feature that again required continual maintenance was the culvert. As the soils sank, they became 'stranded' and had to be lowered or completely rebuilt.

A particular feature of the Fenland railways was the outward leaning of signal posts, telegraph poles and platelayer's huts as the sides of the embankments fell away into the lower lying drained land. Another common feature of these lines was, and is, the number of level crossings, necessary because of the difficulties in building bridges on the Fenland soils. Some said there was another strange feature. The heavy trains tended to run differently on the soft fen soils when compared to hard ground. Others said that there was a different noise, that there was a tendency to rock, causing uneven wear on the edges of the rails and that very heavy locomotives caused a very small moving 'wave' in the track in front of them. Some of these aspects were affected even more by wet, winter or dry, summer conditions.

(See colour section for larger photo)

In spite of these difficulties a comprehensive network of railways, with major junctions at Ely, March and Wisbech, rapidly developed within The Great Level. It was already surrounded by railways. To the west lay the Great Northern railway between London and Edinburgh, to the north the Midland and Great Northern Railway from the Midlands to Norfolk, to the east the Great Eastern Railway from King's Lynn to Swaffham and Thetford and to the south the Great Eastern and Great Eastern and Midland Joint Railway from Cambridge to Huntingdon.

The main north to south route was, and still is, the line from King's Lynn to Denver, Ely and Cambridge built in the 1840s by the East Anglian Railway Company, later to become the Great Eastern Railway. Between King's Lynn and Denver at Magdalen Road, a spur to Wisbech was opened in 1845. It was closed to all traffic in September 1968. At Denver a spur ran east to Stoke Ferry. It was opened in August 1882 and remained in service until April 1965. Midway along this line at Abbey, another spur ran right into the heart of the Fens.

Known as the Wissington Light Railway, it was opened in 1906, without any Act of Parliament or Light Railway Order, for the benefit of local farms. Initially it ran from Abbey for 16km to its terminus at Poppylot between Southery and Feltwell. Some of its rails were second hand, flat bottomed and dated 1883 from Krupps, in Essen. In 1925 it was extended by 13km further into the Fens to ensure the transportation of adequate supplies of sugar beet to the new sugar factory at Wissington. During the Second World War it became of strategic importance to the country. Its management was taken over by the Ministry of Agriculture in 1941 and it was reconditioned by Italian prisoners of war. Despite there being right angled bends, no telephone and no signals, there were trains of up to 100 trucks of local produce. They were hauled by three small steam engines, two pulling at the front and one pushing at the back. The Ministry purchased the line in 1947 and continued to run it until 1957 when all lines beyond the sugar factory were closed. This line too was finally closed in April 1965.

Not only does the King's Lynn to Cambridge line pass through Ely, but a number of former Great Eastern lines radiated from it. To the north-east is the line to Norwich built in 1845. It is on the stretch near Prickwillow that the shrinkage of the Fens is very apparent, the land level being some 2m below the embankment. To the south-east is the line to Ipswich and Bury St Edmunds. It was on this line in 1944 that Soham was almost destroyed. The driver of a 51-wagon ammunition train noticed that the first wagon was on fire. He and his fireman uncoupled the wagon and tried to pull it through the station into open country. However after a few hundred meters, it exploded killing the fireman and a nearby signal man, severely injuring the driver, wrecking the station and destroying over 750 houses, some up to 1km away. The shock was felt for over 30km around.

To the south-west was another Fenland line to St Ives. Known as the Ely, Haddenham and Sutton Railway, the section between Ely and Sutton was opened in April 1866 and the remainder in May 1878. Although there was little passenger traffic, it was an important line for transporting not only local produce but also coal. Because of limited weight and therefore size of engines, and a statutory speed limit of 24km per hour, the journey time was long; about 44 minutes for the 28km. This line was finally closed in October 1958.

With the inherent problems of building railways in the Fens, Earith seems a strange place at which to experiment with rail travel. However it was here that in the early 1970s, that the National Research Development Corporation planned to build a 30km, 1.2m high mono rail-track parallel to and to the west of the Old Bedford River. This was to carry an experimental tracked hovercraft train powered by linear induction motors and which, on a cushion of air, would reach speeds of 480km/hr. The first train, RTV 31, ran along the first 1.6km on December 1, 1971 at a speed of 32km/hr. In spite of reaching a speed of 172km/hour, its potential was never fully realised and the project was scrapped due to lack of funds in 1974.

The fourth route to radiate from Ely was, and is, the line to March, itself a junction for many lines. This line continues west to Whittlesey and Peterborough. It had a spur, opened in August 1898 to Benwick for goods traffic, principally coal and local produce. Only 8km long and having a 24km/hour speed limit, it was closed in July 1964. Passing north to south through March was the former Great Northern and Great Eastern Joint Railway from Wisbech to Chatteris, Bluntisham and St Ives. Known first as the Wisbech, St Ives and Cambridge Junction Railway, it was opened in February 1848 and remained so until March 1967. It was a busy route which avoided Ely, with its passenger expresses, and enabled long, slow, heavy coal trains from the East Midlands to travel south to London. Finally running north-west from March was the former Great Northern and Great Eastern Joint Railway to Spalding.

March became somewhat of a railway town. It had a large locomotive depot where engines from the North-West, the Midlands and North changed with those from East Anglia. It also had one of the biggest mechanised marshalling yards in the country, with over 100km of track, at Whitemoor, now better known for its prison. Its Victorian Gothic railway station decorated with curly cast iron brackets, with leaf and rosette ornaments, is a testament to those great railway days.

Besides being connected to March and to the King's Lynn to Ely and Cambridge line, Wisbech was roughly in the middle of the former Midland and Great Northern Joint Railway from Sutton Bridge to Peterborough. Known first as the Peterborough, Wisbeach (sic) and Sutton Railway, it was opened in 1866 and passed north of Guyhirn and through Thorney. It was closed to all traffic in 1966.

One of the most interesting Fenland 'railways' ran from Wisbech to Outwell and Upwell. It was the Wisbech and Upwell Tramway, a standard-gauge light railway built by the Great Eastern Railway, opened in two stages; first from Wisbech to Outwell in August 1883 and then extended to Upwell in September 1884. The venture to bring rail transport to areas which would be uneconomic to serve with a proper railway was supported by the Board of Trade. Its cost was £2,284 per mile (£114,200 at February 2002), one quarter the cost of a typical branch line. The original special locomotives, small four-wheeled squat tank engines, were designed by Thomas Worsdell and in 1903, larger six wheeled engines, designed by James Holden were introduced. All the engines were required by law to have their wheels and motion protected by a skirting, to have a bell, and to carry a 'cow-catcher'. They were painted in teak and brown colours and looked rather like a steaming and smoking guard's van. Indeed they became the model for one of the Rev. W. Audrey's engines, *No 7, Toby the Tram Engine.* They remained on duty until 1953, when two diesel locomotives took over. The journey was subject to various maximum speed limits, the top being 19kph (limited by governors) and which was lowered to 4.5kph when crossing roads. Consequently the 10km journey took about 40 minutes. However it often took longer as passengers could flag the train down at any point in addition to the official stopping places. The line was finally closed in May 1966.

The arrival of a bus service which delivered its passengers directly to the market instead of 1km away resulted in the loss of this passenger service. Prior to the drainage of Fenland, roads were few and far between not withstanding the Roman Fen Road passing through the north of the Great Level and Akeman Street between Cambridge and King's Lynn. Indeed in the mid-17th century there was no road between Ely and Chatteris. Until Ireton's Way, named after Henry Ireton, Deputy Governor of Ely, and now the A142, was built in 1643, all traffic would have been waterborne. Amongst other things the Lynn Law also required roads and bridges to be built. Robert Morden's map of Cambridgeshire, c1695, illustrates the lack of Fenland roads very well. The only roads which it shows are those actually on the Fenland Islands, the few causeways leading to them, Ireton's Way from the Isle of Ely at Mepal to Chatteris with its northern extension to March and Wisbech and another road from Earith through Somersham also to Chatteris. The condition of this latter road was described in 1667 as 'being in a way very dangerous and not passable'. (In Darby). By the 18th century contemporary maps show a significant change. Watercourses which had previously simply been known as Drains e.g. Vermuyden's Drain, had become Drain and Drove e.g. Vermuyden's Drain and Drove. A network of Droves following the drains and dykes, emerged.

At the end of the 18th century the roads were described as relatively safe and there was a daily return stage-coach between Cambridge and Ely. However poor conditions were to continue. In 1813 it was noted that 'most roads running through the Fens are frequently impassable, even the turnpike one from Downham to Wisbech, not excepted; the "mending" being only the silt, viz, a sand formerly left by the sea, and not a stone amongst it'. (In Darby). It was not until 1821 that the coach service from Cambridge to Ely was extended to King's Lynn. In 1845, the night journey across the Fens between Ely and Dowhham Market, about 25km, took one hour fifty minutes. The last years of coaching on this route, 1846 and 1847, saw the introduction of the Red Rover, a daily long distance coach travelling from London to Cambridge, Ely, King's Lynn and Wells Next the Sea.

Even up to the 1930s, such roads as there were had virtually no foundations. Consequently they were still rutted, boggy and often almost impassable. Sometimes they were straight, but with sudden right angled bends, following old droveways lying beside drainage dykes or consequent upon Enclosures. At other times they were winding and tortuous, lying on the old river beds or their rodhams. Perforce many were 'improved' with a slab of concrete during the 1940s, thus enabling the Fenland produce to be moved to the railways or direct to the towns. This wartime improvement had almost as great an impact on Fenland people as had the drainage 300 years earlier.

In the 21st century whilst their top surface may have improved, their layout remains essentially as it had been. Like the railways their sides tend to slip and slope towards the lower land, causing cracking and an unpleasant feeling of being drawn to the edge. Whilst road signs of bends, double bends, an uneven surface or a neighbouring watercourse should never be ignored, in Fenland in particular, they do really mean what they say. Sadly they are ignored by some. It is not an infrequent occurrence for vehicles and their passengers to end up in the deep dykes and ditches which border the roads.

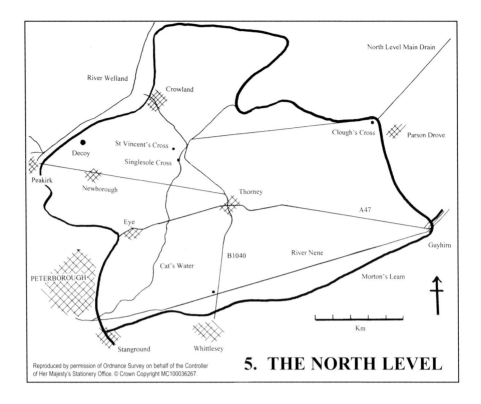

5. THE NORTH LEVEL

The map of the Great Level of the Fens surveyed by Sir Jonas Moor and published in 1708 in *Magna Britannia et Hibernia, Antiqua et Nova*, defines a boundary of the North Level. Its southern boundary between Peterborough and Guyhirn is Morton's Leam. At Guyhirn the boundary turns north and then west along the South Eau Bank. After about 8km, it turns north-east, west and south along the Welland Bank to Crowland, thus surrounding Great Postland. It continues alongside the Welland Bank south-west to Peakirk. Here it turns east and then south, passing to the east of Peterborough, following the line of the Car Dyke to Stanground and so back to Morton's Leam. The east west line of the former Peakirk Drain, now mirrored in the minor road between Peakirk and Thorney, the B 1141, and its extension to Guyhirn, the A 47 trunk road, divides the region in two roughly equal parts. These in turn are divided in two by the north south line of the former north eastern branch of the River Nene, the Cat's Water. It is noteworthy that the River Nene rises at Catesby in Northamptonshire.

Starting in the north-eastern section, Guyhirn is at the extreme eastern point of the North Level where the south-east and north-east sections meet. It is also where the Peakirk Drain, now reflected in the A47 Trunk Road, Morton's Leam and the River Nene meet. Whilst there are now only a few Victorian brick-built houses lying under the flood bank, Guyhirn had an

46

earlier importance. Its name 'Guide Corner' may indicate a junction of rivers. Its small church of St Mary Magdalene, which was designed by Sir George Gilbert Scott and consecrated in 1878, lies on the site of a 14th/15th century chantry chapel, presumably destroyed at the Dissolution. Its strategic importance to the 17th century drainers is reflected in a small, simple, rectangular, grey stone building with square mullioned windows. Dated 1660, bearing the initials RP and funded from money left for that purpose in 1651, it was probably a non-conformist Free Church.

A few kilometres to the north is Parson's Drove and just outside the boundary, Church End. Although described by Samuel Pepys (in Storey) as a 'Heathen Place, where I found my uncle and aunt Perkins and their daughters, poor wretches, in a sad poor thatched cottage like a barn in a stable', these are well named. In the settlements, much of which was destroyed in a flood in 1613, are the Emmanuel Church 1872, a Wesleyan Chapel 1834, the Chapel of Corpus Christi 1857, and the redundant Church of St John which dates from the 13th century and which has a remarkable 15th century west tower. This church perhaps reflects the area's earlier prosperity brought about by the silt, as opposed to peat, fens. One of the industries was the 200 year old business of producing dye from the blue green plant, woad. In one of the last woad mills, worked by a horse, the plants' leaves were crushed and then moulded into balls which were then dried. After about three months, they were mixed with water and left to ferment in the dark for about six weeks, thus producing the dye.

Amongst the curiosities is a brick built building (1876?) which served in part as a war memorial, in part as the previous fire station and in part as a school to serve a scattered community. It proclaims the name 'Parson Drove' on a board above the double doors and is topped by a clock which, instead of numerals, has the words 'Sixty Years On'. There is also the motto 'Virtue Over Death Survives'.

Clough's Cross lies just to the north of Parson Drove on a number of ancient and modern waterways. The South Eau Bank and Lady Nun's Old Eau lie on the ancient course of one of the branches of the River Nene. The New South Eau (1631) from St Vincent's Cross turns into the North Level Main Drain (1831–4) which discharges into the River Nene between Tydd St Mary and Walpole St Mary.

St Vincent's Cross, marking the former boundary between the Abbeys of Crowland and Thorney, together with the remains of another cross at Singlesole Farm, the site of St Michael's Chapel, lie just within the north-west part of the North Level, although Singlesole Farm itself is actually in the north-east portion.

Crowland is in the north-west part of the region. It has a certain atmosphere. An old legend (in Storey) tells how William the Conqueror gave permission for the body of Waltheof, Earl of Northumberland to be buried there. Waltheof, a benefactor of the Abbey and husband of Judith, William's niece, had become too greedy and over-ambitious. Despite gaining the King's favour in 1070, he was beheaded at Winchester in 1076. Before long pilgrims, thinking him to be a great and good man visited his grave. In an attempt to prove or refute this belief, his coffin was opened up in about 1088. His body was found to be totally unblemished and his head was rejoined to his body, only a thin scar showing where the executioner's bade had struck. In a similar vein, the skull of Abbot Theodore, slain at the altar by the Danes, was displayed for years in a glass case fixed to one of the pillars of the Aisle. There was a large hole in the skull.

At the Dissolution of the Monasteries, the transepts and chancel of the Benedictine Abbey were destroyed. The remainder, except for the north nave aisle which had become the parish church, decayed to form a spectacular ruin, the subject of many paintings.

Marlowe tells of a relatively modern legend concerning a lady artist from London. It is said that she stayed with a local farmer, his wife and a young widow who assisted the farmers in return for free board and lodging. This widow had the strange habit of furtively eating raw meat instead of cooked meat. One day after a day's sketching, as the artist returned home in the evening gloom, the young widow suddenly appeared. The artist was glad for her company and they continued together along the lonely road. After a while the artist realised that the widow had fallen behind her. She said she would catch up and so the artist continued in the deepening gloom. However as the widow had not moved, the artist started to go back thinking perhaps she was ill. Suddenly the form of the widow dropped to the ground and began bounding towards her like a wolf after her blood. Just before the wolf sprang at her throat, the artist grabbed her torch and shone its bright beam straight into the wolf's eyes, whereupon the wolf seemed to shrivel up and vanish in a cloud of smoke.

The artist fled back to the farmhouse only to find there a scene of confusion. About half an hour before her return, the widow, who had been in the farmhouse all evening, had fallen to the ground screaming 'my eyes, my eyes'. As she appeared to have been blinded the doctor was called. He found that her eyes had been burnt as if by lightning. There had been no lightning that night. Perhaps amongst the demons that St Guthlac saw, there were also Werewolves.

There is a sobering tablet to an Abrm. Baly, 1706.

> *'Man's life is like unto a winter's day,*
> *some break their fast and so departs away;*
> *others stay dinner then departs full fed,*
> *the longest age but sups and goes to bed.*
> *O Reader, then behold and see;*
> *as we are now so must you be.'*

In the middle of Crowland is an unusual triangular bridge, Trinity Bridge. It is somewhat of an enigma. Whilst it is thought to have been built in the late 13th or early 14th century, an anonymous author writing about bridges in 1839, dates it at 860. Although three roads met there, the bridge was too steep and narrow for anyone to cross other than by foot. Some suggest the arches had no purpose other than to support a cross. Defoe on the other hand wrote that the bridge was at the meeting place of tributaries of the Rivers

Nene and Welland, which met here. Whilst this is probably the most accurate reason, he also referred to a superstition that there was a whirlpool or bottomless pit at the crossing.

Upstream and close to the Welland in Borough Fen, is one of the finest remaining duck decoys, dating from 1640. Originating in Holland they were devices for luring wild fowl as opposed to driving them. They consisted of a pool, perhaps a few acres in size, around which there were a number, generally eight, of radiating pipes or channels. Tame ducks, trained to paddle up these pipes, were kept on the pool. As they travelled up the pipes they were followed by wild fowl, which in turn were captured by the hidden 'decoyman'. Defoe noted a decoy near Ely from which 3,000 brace a week were sent to London.

Continuing clockwise, through the four areas, immediately south of the road dividing the original Borough Fen and dividing the north-west and south-west parts of this Level is Newborough and (now) Newborough Fen. It was built as a village for farmers and small holders who had been displaced by the Enclosures. Its church, built in 1821, had been paid for by selling land to the north in Borough Fen.

Eye, on the edge of brickworks, lies to the south-east of Newborough. Meaning a land surrounded by marsh or water, it was built on a gravel ridge along one main east west street. Almost all of the early houses here were destroyed by a fire in November 1848. A road passes north to south through the village from Crowland towards Stanground. It must have been of some importance since a number of ancient properties or sites lie next to it. To the north is Northholm Farm dating from 1704. To the south Eyebury Farm lies on the site of a house previously belonging to the Abbot of Peterborough. The moated Oxney House, further to the south, is on the site of a grange of the Abbey of Peterborough.

Further to the south is Flag Fen, site of an ancient settlement. In 1982, during some routine drainage ditch maintenance, some evidently old, worked timbers were discovered. Subsequent radiocarbon dating placed them at 1000 BC. The excavations which followed revealed five rows of posts dating from between 1350 BC and 950 BC. Stretching for over 1km, they formed a vast palisade which contained a total of some 60,000 posts surrounded by a timber platform. That the site survived at all is due to waterlogging and the timbers are now preserved, submerged in large water tanks.

The site has been developed into a national Bronze and Iron Age centre. It contains both a reconstructed Bronze Age roundhouse and a later Iron Age roundhouse, both based on those excavated nearby at Fengate in 1972. The site also houses the timbers removed for future preservation from Sea Henge at Holme next the Sea in Norfolk. Of particular interest is the upside down oak stump which occupied the centre of this early Bronze Age timber circle.

(See colour section for larger photo)

Continuing south into the south-east portion of the North Level, Stanground lies at the entrance of the River Nene and Morton's Leam into Fenland. Like Flag Fen, right on the edge of Fenland, evidence of early occupation has been found. A Bronze Age wooden dug-out canoe was discovered in 1828 and the village was mentioned in a land grant made in 952 by King Elfwin. It was passed to the Abbots of Thorney who were the patrons of the early 14th century church of St John the Baptist. In its grave-yard is the 12th century (?) Lampass Cross. It originally stood a little to the south, at the junction of the Farcet and Whittlesey roads. For a time it served as a footbridge across a dyke, before being moved to the vicarage for safe keeping and then finally (?) to the grave-yard.

At Dog in a Doublet lock, just to the west of the Whittlesey to Thorney Road, the River Nene becomes tidal. The name 'Dog in a Doublet' is derived from the inn on the north bank. An old inn sign may have provided a clue to the derivation of its name. On one side a huntsman was shown with a dog looking out from his doublet. On the other side was a picture of a dog dressed in a doublet. The Whittlesey Washes lie between this river and Morton's Leam. They provide about 1,500ha of flood storage, and, when conditions are right, a traditional area for skating. In the 18th century a local blacksmith made the skates known as 'Whittlesey Runners' and which were the standard skates in the Fen races up to the 1890s.

About 2km downstream there is a significant kink in the River Nene called Popley's (or Popely's or Abel's) Gull. In the 18th century the river banks were weakened, probably due to the 'haling' horses. Consequently, between 1760 and 1770, there were a number of breaches, or 'Gulls'. Their repair often left kinks breaking the straight line of the river; Popley's Gull is the site of one such breach.

A passenger ferry service operated from Peterborough along the River Nene to Dog in a Doublet, and thence north along the Thorney River, passing west of Toneham to Thorney. Long after the demise of the Abbey, Thorney, now standing some 5m above the surrounding Fenland, became an estate village. In what was described as 'the most successful experiment in social organisation that England has so far seen', (in Scarfe), the Duke of Bedford set up between 1830 and 1860, an entire community for his workers. As he believed they would be happy and healthy if properly housed, he built, flanking the High Street, rows of houses of differing sizes according to their occupants' standing. For their health he supplied running water and a sewerage system. On the top, fifth, floor of the massive water tower (1855) which dominates the village, was the fresh water tank. Immediately below, on the fourth floor, was a tank into which sewage was pumped and held prior to its disposal. For their education he supplied a reading room and a lecture room. Justifiably he claimed 'no tenant evicted, excellent public health, minimal crime, no pauperism', (in Scarfe).

The Middle Level lies to the south of Morton's Leam.

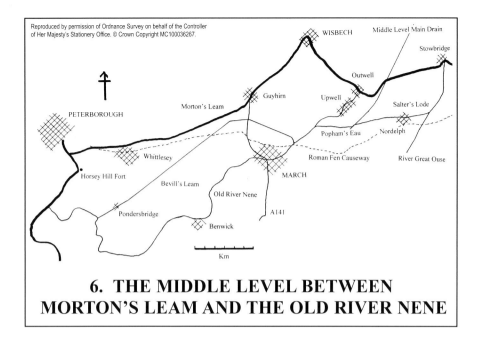

6. THE MIDDLE LEVEL BETWEEN MORTON'S LEAM AND THE OLD RIVER NENE

The north-west boundary of the Middle Level between Wisbech and Stanground lies along the River Nene as far as Guyhirn and then lies along Morton's Leam. To the east and south, rising ground between Stanground, Yaxley, Holme, Wood Walton, Warboys, Somersham and Earith, forms a natural boundary. The south-east boundary from Earith follows the Old Bedford River to Denver and then the tidal River Great Ouse to Stowbridge. From Stowbridge, the northern boundary follows the line of the Old Podyke Bank to Outwell and then the course of the ancient Welle Stream back to Wisbech.

This district can also be divided into four sections. The principal east to west dividing line runs from Salter's Lode, at the junction of Well Creek and the River Great Ouse, to Yaxley. Its course is along Well Creek, Popham's Eau, and the course of the Old River Nene, passing through March, and to the north of Ramsey. The north to south dividing line runs from Guyhirn on the junction of Morton's Leam and the River Nene, south along the old road, also through March, to Doddington, Wimblington, and Chatteris. After Chatteris it continues south along the course of the Old West River to Earith.

Stowbridge, with its inn, the Heron and large 17th century 'Dutch' brick built house lies on the tidal River Great Ouse at the north-east corner of the north-east section of the Middle Level. About 5.5km to the south is Salter's Lode lock which enables boats to pass between the Great Ouse and the Middle Level navigation. It is a tricky lock and passage should only be undertaken after consultation with the lock keeper. This lock was, according

to Dougdale, 'a great sasse on Welle Creek' (sasse-lock). The present lock, guarded by a fine pair of stone eagles, dates from 1827 and cost around £7,000 (£275,500 at February 2002) to build. The small hamlet of Salter's Lode became established around the lock.

Nordelph, 3km to the east at the junction of Well Creek and Popham's Eau, was important at two distinct times. First it was a large Romano-British village lying close to the Roman Fen Causeway. Secondly between the mid-16th century and mid-19th century, it became important as it lay at a key meeting point of fen drains and navigable rivers. Indeed before it had its own church of Holy Trinity (1865), its parishioners used to travel by horse drawn barge along Well Creek to church at Outwell. On their way they might have passed the remains of Mullicourt Priory. Although no trace remains now, it was probably a 10th century Benedictine Priory annexed to Ely. Its name however is preserved in the iron Mullicourt Aqueduct which carries Well Creek over the Middle Level Main Drain.

Just to the south of Upwell, Three Holes became another important place positioned as it was in the middle of Popham's Eau and the Sixteen Foot Drain (1651) and its extension into the Middle Level Main Drain (1845). The nearby strangely named Euximoor Fen is derived from the 15th century Yekeswellemoor, supposedly meaning 'the marsh by the cuckoo's spring or stream'. Close by is the site of the 13th century Gilbertine Priory at Marmont. Following deep ploughing, no trace now remains, although its name is preserved as Marmont Priory lock.

Upwell and Outwell in effect form a single village, as indeed it was in the Middle Ages: Welle. At that time to distinguish between the two ends of what was the longest village in England, it was divided into Upwell, the upstream end and Outwell, the outflowing end. They lay on the old course of the Welle Stream which forms the boundary between Cambridgeshire to the west and Norfolk to the east. Both of the churches lie in Norfolk. The combined villages became important in the 14th century when traders in Northamptonshire preferred the route east to the sea at King's Lynn as opposed to Wisbech. They also preferred the route through March, Upwell, Outwell and along the Welle Stream to the Great Ouse as opposed to the longer route down the Old Croft River via Welney to the River Great Ouse at Littleport.

Upwell's church of St Peter, dates from the 13th century, and like many Fenland churches, its roof appears supported by angels, in this case large with spread wings. It contains a very salutary memorial:

'In memory of sixty seven individuals of various ages and either sex who in the short period from June 21st to August 13th AD 1832 died in this Rectory of Asiatic Cholera, a disease frightful and previously unknown in this country. Reader why hast thou been spared? To what purpose hast thou been left until now?'

Outwell's mid-13th century church of St Clement also has its roof supported, this time by angels with red wings. One of them carries a scroll inscribed with an anchor for St Clement. He was the third Bishop of Rome who was allegedly banished to the Crimea, which he then converted to Christianity, before being drowned with an anchor tied around his neck.

Just to the north of Outwell, on the way to Elm, is the site of Beaupré Hall (1525) and Beaupré Hall Farm, a red brick Jacobean house with stepped gable ends.

Elm, with its many nearby Roman settlements at which have been found an altar, coins, and ware, was known in the 10th century as Eolum, suggesting Eels. In the early 14th century it lay in a land described as 'terra morosa et marisci'. Continuing on this theme it is said that in the vicarage drawing room, the ghost of a monk who forgot to ring the flood warning bell, has been seen. Its 13th century church of All Saints may mark the next stage of Fen reclamation following the Roman's departure. The Early English tower almost appears squat despite being over 20m high. Inside the roof is not only supported by angels, but there are carved reliefs depicting recumbent nudes, dragons, mermaids, rowing boats, swan, pelican, wildfowl, the fable of the lion and the ape, foliage and flowers and other patterns.

Elm now lies on the outskirts of Wisbech, the part of which was bounded by the Old Welle Stream and the River Nene, lay within the Middle Level as previously defined. Although it grew up in the junction between these two rivers, it is possible that the original settlement of Wisbech (Wis-water, becc-stream) lay just on the west side of the River Nene. The Old Market was known as such as early as 1221 and thus would suggest a very early trading centre.

The castle however was built in the apex in the late 11th century or early 12th century. Some say it was built by William 1, others say it was built by one of the Bishops of Ely to whom the Manor of Wisbech had passed in 1109. King John is said to have stayed here on the night he was told he had lost his treasure. It was well positioned to control not only the rivers but also movement around the Wash. At that date Wisbech lay on the coast. It also had the effect of encouraging the town to migrate east across the river and come under its protection. The parish church of St Peter and St Paul, the earliest parts of which date from c1150 was built under its walls. The castle has long since vanished however its Bailey Ditch is reflected in the curving line of the High Street and the Crescent follows the line of its stone walls.

Because of its relative inaccessibility, it made a good prison. Early prisoners included Robert the Bruce's wife and his two daughters. Its role changed slightly when, between 1473 and 1478, Bishop Morton built his palace on the castle site. Despite this change of use, it still served as a prison. Amongst the later prisoners were Robert Catesby and Francis Tresham, the 'Gunpowder Plotters' and Bishop Thomas Watson (1513–1584), one of Mary Tudor's Bishops. He was there for 28 years, having spoken rather incautiously about excommunicating Queen Elizabeth. Others, such as William Wolsey and Robert Piggot, were held there before being burnt at the stake or dying in capture for their beliefs.

During Cromwell's time the site was sold to his Secretary of State, Sir John Thurloe (1616–1668) and he had a house designed by Inigo Jones and built with materials from the former palace. After the Restoration it was handed back to the Bishops of Ely who held it until 1792, when it was purchased by Joseph Meredith. It was he who demolished any other remains, including Thurloe's house, and between 1803 and 1816, built the crescent.

Life for Wisbech as a port started in Roman times when both the River Nene and River Great Ouse flowed directly out to the sea. Since that time however the port has had a chequered history primarily due to the continual siltation (and associated flooding) problems in the estuary. At times this prevented all but the smallest ships reaching the town. Around 1300 the River Great Ouse was diverted from to its present course and outfall at King's Lynn. At the same time the Welle Stream became, to a certain extent, a lesser watercourse. The consequent reduction in flow out to the sea at Wisbech led to a deteriorating situation. Little was done until the construction of Morton's Leam which did lead to an increase in flow and thus trade. Whilst this trade was reasonable in the mid-16th century, it had declined again by the early 17th century. Vermuyden built a sluice just downstream of the town in 1631 as well as a 4km cut, both aimed at reducing siltation and increasing navigation. By the early 18th century the town was becoming established as a major port, however later that century not only were there disastrous floods, but the siltation problems had returned. More remedial measures were taken in 1773 in the shape of Kinderley's Cut and again in 1830 in the form of the Nene Outfall Cut designed by Rennie and Telford. Although there was a slight decline in business following the introduction of the railway in 1847, Wisbech has served as a port until the end of the 20th century when operations were moved downstream to Sutton Bridge.

(See colour section for larger photo)

It was during the prosperous periods, particularly during the 18th century and early 19th century, that the great houses were built in Wisbech, notably those lining the river banks, the North Brink and South Brink, and in the Crescent. Arguably the finest is Peckover House on the North Brink. It is believed to have been built in c1722 and bought by Joseph Peckover towards the end of that century. In 1877 Alexander Peckover, a former Lord Lieutenant of Cambridgeshire, added two wings. In 1948 it was handed over to the National Trust.

It is perhaps fitting that the house should now be owned by the National Trust, since on the opposite bank in the South Brink, is the birth place of Octavia Hill (1834–1912). She was much interested in housing reform, social reform and preservation. It was she who together with Sir Robert Hunter (1844–1913), a solicitor and authority on common and public rights, and Canon Rawnsley, founded the National Trust in 1895.

Wisbech's most famous son is arguably Thomas Clarkson (1760–1846). The son of a local school master, he became interested in human liberty. He became friendly with Granville Sharp and William Wilberforce and on 22 May 1787 joined a committee for the suppression of the slave trade. At that time seldom less than 50% and often more than 80% of the slaves died in transit; many of those that survived became blind. He inspected ships seeking evidence and witnesses. He spoke throughout the country as well as to the French government and the Tsar of Russia. He assisted in founding the Anti Slavery Society and eventually he saw the abolition of slavery. He was made a Freeman of the City of London in 1839.

On receiving a congratulatory ode from Bernard Barton, his wife was asked to write a reply. She said she would 'treasure the verses up for herself; but her good man was so little of a poetical amateur that when he had received a similar tribute once forwarded to him in the form of an ode, the poet was forced to promise him a prose translation'. (In Meredith). Today he stands on his 13m high monument designed by Sir Gilbert Scott looking down on his town. Underneath him and his memorial are brick barrel vaults dating from the early Tudor period.

The Middle Level seems to have been a favourite place for the development of Co-operative Societies. One such, the Wisbech United Advancement Society was founded by James Hill, a banker and father of Octavia Hill, in 1832. He planned that there should be 400 members each paying 6d (£1 at February 2002) per week into a fund that would be used to purchase c4ha (10 acres) of land for cultivation. The landholders were enabled to buy produce cheaply and these monies were to be put in a general fund to purchase other necessities. An estate was purchased in 1839, however the venture failed and broke up completely when James Hill died in 1856.

Before leaving Wisbech it has to be said that Lord Orford was not the only one to have a whale. Apparently Wisbech had one too. When Hilaire Belloc visited, 'he read in a book descriptive of the place, that a whale had come up from Wisbeach [sic] once, and I considered that a whale coming up to Wisbeach on a tide would certainly stay there; not indeed for the delights of the town (of which I say nothing) but because there would be no room to turn round; and a whale can not swim backwards'. (in Meredith).

Returning south towards March, the road passes through Friday Bridge and Coldham. Needham Hall near Friday Bridge was the site of a medieval aisled hall. Oliver Cromwell is said to have slept here on an oak table 'so that he should be no better lodged than his soldiers' (in Manning). Friday Bridge's Victorian church has a leaning tower; indeed not only it is leaning but it has also pulled the whole of the west end into the peat; even the font is crooked.

Although March is at the centre of the four parts of the Middle Level, the northern part lies clearly in the north-east section. Straddling the Roman Fen Causeway which ran to the north of the town, was one of the largest mechanised marshalling and sorting yards for railway wagons in the country; Whitemoor. Works in 1929 and 1933 resulted in over 80km of track as sidings, and over 2,000 associated jobs were created. Whitemoor lay not only at the centre of a network of railways, but it also lay between the industrial north and midlands and the agricultural south and south-east. The goods trains were broken up and sorted by pushing the wagons up over humps, down which they rolled along a 1:18 gradient onto the chosen tracks which fanned out below. The sidings are no more; the northern part of the site is occupied by H. M. Prison Whitemoor.

The Roman Fen Causeway continues through Westry, on the west side of March, to Eldernell, Coates, and Eastrea, on the east side of Whittlesey. Both Coates and Whittlesey were amongst the first of the Fenland Isles to come into Christendom, being granted c657 to Sexwulf, the first Abbot of Peterborough.

Whilst Wisbech's sons and daughters leant towards social reform, Whittlesey's sons were of a military disposition. Harry Smith, or more precisely Lieutenant General Sir Harry George Wakelyn Smith Bart., was born in 1788 in Aliwal House in St Mary's Street. He won his KCB during the Sikh British war during the third battle of the war which was a decisive victory for him. The Anglo Indian army had pushed the Sikhs back to the Sutlej River at Aliwal in the East Punjab. On 28 January 1846, Sir Harry with some 10,000 men charged an enemy force about twice as large as his own. On the third charge he routed the enemy. Two weeks later he brought the war to an end by winning the Battle of Sobraon. He went on to become Governor of the Cape of Good Hope and the South African towns of Harrysmith, Whittlesey and Ladysmith are named after him, his birthplace and his wife. He died in 1860 and is buried in St Mary's church.

A market town for over seven centuries, Whittlesey formerly Witelsig or Witsie, after a Saxon landowner Whitel, is now almost surrounded by the industrial landscape arising from the long established brick industry. As a contrast its parish church of St Mary has one of the most splendid towers in the county (c1450). The church itself dates from 1244. Wisbech's other church of St Andrew was appropriated to the Presenter of Ely by Bishop Nigel (1133–1169) to increase Ely's funds for writing and acquiring books. Nothing of that date remains. One William Whittlesey was to become Archbishop of Canterbury from 1368 until his death in 1374. He is said to have protested at St Paul's against taxation. He started his sermon only to collapse and be taken by boat to Lambeth where he died soon after.

If Wisbech had its whale, Whittlesey has its bears. In the recently revived custom, there is Straw Bear Dancing. On Straw Bear Tuesday, the day after Plough Monday, a man completely covered in straw, is led around the town by a piece of rope and made to dance in front of houses for money.

The western approaches to Whittlesey and thus across the Fens to King's Lynn were guarded by the mid-17th century Horsey Hill Fort, built on Horsey Hill all of 7m above sea level. It was of pentagonal construction having five bastions for cannon. A gatehouse and three houses were positioned inside the earth bank, the latter presumably being barracks for the garrison.

The road south from Whittlesey passes through Pondersbridge on Bevill's Leam (1631) to Ramsey St Mary. This parish was formed in c1860 following drainage of the surrounding land. Its church once had a tower however it had to be taken down because fen shrinkage caused it lean. The road continues south across the old course of the River Nene into the south-western section of the Middle Level which lies between the old course of the River Nene and the Old Bedford River.

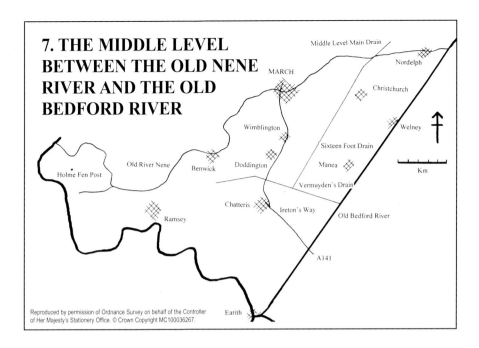

7. THE MIDDLE LEVEL BETWEEN THE OLD NENE RIVER AND THE OLD BEDFORD RIVER

Holme Fen is at the western edge of the south-western section of the Middle Level, lying just to the south of the old course of the River Nene. During the Middle Ages, Holme developed as a minor port and by 1314 it had been granted a market and two fairs. However silting up of the River Nene estuary and the cutting of Morton's Leam led to its decline during the 16th century.

About 2km north-east are the Holme Fen Posts described in Chapter 3. They are situated right on the edge of the former Whittlesey Mere, originally the largest of the Fenland Meres including Trundle Mere, Ugg Mere and Ramsey Mere. Much has been found in it including a wooden dug-out canoe and following draining in 1853, a silver incense censer and a chandelier. A symbolic ram's head suggest they came from Ramsey Abbey.

Some 4km by 2.5km and occupying between 400ha and 640ha depending upon the season, it was, in the 18th century and early 19th century a great place for watersports. In the summer these included regattas, sailing, rowing, fishing, and general enjoyment. There were boat houses, a band stand and refreshment houses built around the edge. In the winter there was sleighing, ice yachting and, of course, skating.

Wood Walton Fen was first established as a nature reserve when about 140ha of Fenland was purchased by the Hon. Charles Rothschild in 1910. He gave this land over to nature conservation after he had purchased additional lands. Today the Fen is run as English Nature's Wood Walton Fen National Nature Reserve. The land has been undrained and now stands above the surrounding Fenland. Stretches of open water are maintained with swamps, reeds, sedge, heath and mixed woodland.

On the very western edge of the Middle Level, Wood Walton grew up as an Iron Age settlement. Its isolated church stands mid-way between the present village and the remains of a castle. Its isolated position suggests it might be on the site of a much earlier building. The remains of the castle indicate a motte and bailey construction, believed to have been built by Geoffrey de Mandeville as an outpost for the garrison which he held in Ramsey in the early 12th century.

Whilst there is evidence of nearby Bronze Age settlements, Ramsey first came to prominence when the Abbey was founded (Chapter 2). During the 12th century the land round about was 'such that the land converted to tillage bears corn plentifully; nor is it less profitable otherwise, being full of fair gardens, rich pasture, shady groves and rich meadows; which in the spring time look most beautiful' (Chronicum Abbatiae Ramesiensis in Summers). It was to this land and to the Abbey that Geoffrey de Mandeville came in c1143. He was the first Earl of Essex and Constable of the Tower of London. Whilst he helped King Stephen to put down insurgents, he was in fact playing a double role, for which he was arrested in 1142. On his release soon after, he went to the Fens and to Ely, after which he went without opposition to Ramsey Abbey. This he took and strengthened as his main garrison. He was fatally wounded on the eastern edge of the Fens, at Burwell Castle, a castle actually being built by King Stephen to contain the rebels. After his death his son returned the Abbey to the monks.

The parish church of St Thomas a Beckett, parts of which date back to the 12th century, may have been the hospitum or guest house of the Abbey. It also may have acted as the parish church since the late 13th century. An inscribed sundial stone over the west door of the tower (1733) offers the advice:

'Take heed, watch and pray, for ye know not what the time is'.

Ramsey developed as a small town and a port became established on the Bury Brook which used to run down the middle of the Great Whyte. It was covered over between 1853 and 1854 and the very wide street is the consequence. The town received a grant of market in c1200 and a fair in 1267. By the mid-18th century the market had become one of the best in England for cattle and wildfowl. Many of the old buildings were however destroyed in two extensive fires during the 18th century, and the fair lost its prominence during the 19th century surviving only as a pleasure fair. Two centuries later the town suffered further extensive damage when a solitary German bomber dropped its load of bombs on the town.

Travelling north towards Benwick, the road passes the very small Fen island of Bodsey. It was gifted to Ramsey Abbey in 969 and remained thus as a rest home for monks until the Dissolution. At the Reformation it came in to Cromwell's hands and he converted it into a partially moated Manor House.

Benwick is an old Fen village, sited not on an island, but on the ancient roddons of the old Rivers Nene and Great Ouse. It came into prominence as the meeting place of these large rivers and is one of the few villages in the Fens to feature in the Doomsday Book. Strategically sited, it too became an outpost of Geoffrey de Mandeville's garrison at Ramsey. It is noteworthy for the manner in which some of its houses lean at startling angles as the roddons slip into the drained Fens. Inside the old parish church of St Mary, now destroyed, the subsidence made it feel like being at sea.

The village inn is 'The Five Alls'. The original inn sign explained:

> *'A lawyer, I pray for all;*
> *a parson, I pray for all;*
> *a soldier, I fight for all;*
> *Queen Victoria, I rule all.'*

And underneath a carving of a workman at the plough
> *'I pay for all.'*

As it flowed from Earith to Benwick, the old River Great Ouse passed west of Chatteris. It is surrounded by Fen barrows and tumuli where a number of Bronze Age, Iron Age and Saxon weapons have been found. In 1824, a hoard of 1,000 Roman coins was ploughed up. The parish church of St Peter and St Paul is mainly 20th century, having been rebuilt by Blomfield. However parts of its nave and west tower are 14th century possibly having survived a great fire in 1310. The town was connected to Vermuyden's Drain by a road and cut and consequently a small port developed in the northern part.

Like Whittlesey it had a famous soldier son; George William Clare VC. During the First World War, when the garrison of an outlying post had fallen, he crossed open ground, swept all the time by heavy gunfire. He dressed all the wounded, manned the post single handed and carried one man to cover under intense fire. When he learnt that the enemy was using gas, he personally warned the surrounding posts of the danger. Eventually he was killed by a shell.

The road leads north, possibly lying on the course of an extinct river, to Doddington, Wimblington and March. Doddington was once at the centre of the largest parish in Cambridgeshire (c15,000ha). It may have had an early Minster church as its parish included seven associated parochial chapelries, four in March, one at Benwick, one at Wimblington and Doddington itself. Subservient to Ely for over 600 years, during the 11th century the Bishops maintained a palace here; nothing of this remains. In 1601 it was given to Sir John Peyton, Lieutenant of the Tower of London and Governor of Jersey and Guernsey. It is said (in Bloom) that one of the Peytons accidentally killed on of his servants. Although it was an accident, he was sentenced to have a blood stained hand painted on all his possessions including on his church pew. Each year he was allowed to have the hand redrawn slightly smaller. A small hand can be seen carved on one of the church's choir stall ends.

Its church of St Mary dates from the mid-13th century and its roof is supported by feathery winged angels. To the north of the churchyard are the remains of a 14th century wayside cross removed there from nearby field by a former rector, for safe keeping. A particular rector was Dr. Christopher Tye (1497?–1572), musician and choir master. Known as 'The Father of

Anthems', he composed many well known hymn tunes including 'Winchester' to which is sung 'While Shepherds watch their flocks'. He is said to have been rebuked by Queen Elizabeth for playing out of tune. He replied that her ears were out of tune (in Mee).

The 19th century William Morris stained glass window was dedicated by Sir Charles Townshend, the 'The Hero of Kut'. In September 1915 he defeated the Turks and captured Kut al Amara. His victory was short lived as he was besieged and forced to surrender following the failure of Sir John Nixon's attempt to relive him.

The southern outskirts of March are reached after passing through Wimblington, a medieval hamlet of Doddington, and which had two guildhalls and a chapel. The name 'March' means boundary, but a boundary of what? Perhaps it was so called because of its position on the northern edge of a Fenland isle around which the ancient River Nene flowed and beyond which open Fenland stretched to the sea. Perhaps it was because of the Roman Fen Causeway which passed just to the north of the town. Perhaps it was because it was an outlying Grange of Ely on the boundary of estates owned by other great Abbeys.

Perhaps it was an outpost of the Devil. When the people of March first started building their church, the Devil, claiming the Fens as his own, pulled down each night everything that had been built. Thinking that the sign of the Cross would drive him away, the people built a stone cross. Their plan worked and whilst the cross remained where it had been built, the church was built elsewhere. The remains of a 14th century wayside cross can be seen lying between the river to the north and the 14th century church of St Wendra to the south. Dedicated to a Saxon Saint and dating from the early 14th century, it has one of the most splendid double hammerbeam roofs in the country. The roof is held up by four tiers of angels, 118 in total, all with outstretched wings. A 'spoiler' or 'cartoon' of a carved 'Prince of Darkness' appears on one spandrel in order to prevent the whole work appearing too perfect. He also keeps the roof moored to the ground! Unusually the tower is supported on arches high enough to allow a carriage to pass underneath; an ancient right-of-way is thus preserved.

After the Roman Occupation, the settlement grew from one with a Doomsday population of just 12, to become over the next 200 years, a small trading port with river and road traffic. It remained as such into the

16th century with a market and two fairs. Three centuries later the railway arrived and the town expanded rapidly. The railways strongly influenced the town. There are inn names such as The Great Northern. There are street names such as Locomotive Street. There are cast iron works such as the Market Place clock commemorating Queen Victoria's Diamond Jubilee and the memorial fountain commemorating the coronation of George V. There is a Victorian Gothic station with cast iron columns, curly brackets and leaf and rosette ornaments. Such was its importance that it became the administrative capital of the Isle of Ely when the Isle was an administrative county.

To the east of March in the south-east section of the Middle Level is the old hamlet of Christchurch, lying on a bend of the Old Croft River. In 1893 Dorothy Sayers, daughter of the Reverend Henry Sayers, vicar of Christchurch, was born. Later the family moved to Bluntisham on the edge of the Fens. Dorothy used these Fenland settings for her famous detective story, The Nine Taylors.

Lying along the Old Croft River 'upstream' from Christchurch is Welney, the village of which lies just within the Middle Level. It was the home of the famous mid-19th century skaters, 'Turkey' Smart, 'Fish' Smart, and 'Gutta Percha' See (so nicknamed for his toughness). Turkey Smart was credited with skating or 'running' a mile in 2 minutes 2 seconds. Turkey was Fen Champion for 10 years and it is said that he always put his winnings safely into a bank. The bank in question was the nearby bank of the Old Bedford River.

Welney is now best known for the Welney Wildfowl and Wetlands trust. The 400ha of traditionally managed washland, which actually lies within the South Level, is known not only for its flowers, reeds, rushes, butterflies and dragonflies, but more importantly for its birds. During the winter thousands of migrating and over wintering wildfowl make it one of the greatest wildlife spectacles in Europe, particularly during the evening feeding.

The ancient sites of Stonea, Honey Hill and Manea lie at the corners of an almost perfect equilateral triangle. Stonea Camp, first recorded in c955, lies on a small gravel island and indeed its name means 'gravely marshland'. From an Iron Age settlement or Hill (!) Fort it grew into a well fortified Roman administrative centre and military post. Honey Hill was once a Romano-British village on a small Fenland Isle, sometimes known as Huna's Island. It was to this spot to which St Huna, chaplain to St Etheldreda, retired after he had buried her. It was his first resting place because his bones were later removed to Thorney after cures had been experienced at his graveside.

Despite, or perhaps because, of its name meaning an island common or common pasture in a well watered land, Manea was to become a strange choice for 'social' proposals and events. The first was a proposal by King Charles 1 to: 'enrich these countries by several new plantations and divers ample privileges; Amongst his royal intentions, that of the building of an eminent town in the middle of the Level, at a little village called Manea and to have it called Charlemont was one: the design whereof he drew himself, intending to have made a navigable stream from thence to the River Ouse' (in Summers). His plans never came to fruition.

Plans which did however come to fruition, albeit for a short time, were proposed in 1838 by William Hudson from Upwell. This 19th century experiment in communal living involved the establishment of a self supporting colony centred on c50ha of nearby Fenland. With its motto 'Each for All', it was to follow the principles of the social reformer and originator of the 'Villages of Unity and Co-operation' scheme, Robert Owen. In the autumn of 1838, 40 single men and 10 married men became the first colonists of the 'Cambridge Community No. 1'. They started building houses and labourers and tradesmen joined the early settlers; soon there were over 200 members. Given no cash for wages, they were given vouchers to change for goods in the community store. They published a periodical called 'The Working Bee' and adopted a uniform of green tunics, trousers and straw hats or caps for the men and tunics for the women. Running into early financial problems, Hudson proposed a plan to market their products on the open market. These plans did not materialise and he resigned as president along with many other members. By 1851 the project had been abandoned. The land which they had worked was flat, very flat, so flat that looking along the nearby railway line it was possible to see the curvature of the earth.

Purls Bridge and Welche's Dam lie a little upstream along the Old Bedford River. At Purls Bridge (Purl-a small stream) there are just a very few houses and the Ship Inn. Not long ago there were two other public houses, the Anchor and the Chequers. They all provided food and lodging for those working on the repair and maintenance of the Middle and South Level Barrier Banks, for those who patrolled the banks looking for signs of leaks, and for passing bargees. Formerly the village had a bigger population, but they had left because of the fear of damp and infection. For example in 1849 there were 11 cases of cholera, so most of the inhabitants moved to the higher (!) village at Mepal.

(See colour section for larger photo)

At one time two of the three houses at Welche's Dam were public houses, The Three Fishes and the Princess Victoria. Now there are just a few cottages, a lock enabling navigation to proceed from the Old Bedford River into the Middle Level, and a large pumping station. The village is named after Edmund Welch who built a dam there to prevent water from Vermuyden's Drain flowing upstream to Earith; hence the kink in the rivers and their apparent change in name.

Between Welche's Dam and Earith, and opposite Byall Fen is Fortrey's Hall. In Scarfe it is told that 'James Fortrey, descended from ancient stock in Brabant which took an asylum in England from the persecution of the Spaniards in the reign of Queen Elizabeth. He was the third son of Samuel Fortrey Esq., who upon undertaking the draining of the Bedford Level, erected a commodious habitation in Byal Fen... Having lived a favourite of four Princes, he... passed the remainder of his days in retirement between Portugal and Byall Fen'.

As defined earlier, the Middle Level land extended beyond Earith to near the tidal limit at Brownshill Staunch. Between Earith and Brownshill is Bury Fen where amateur, professional, national and international ice skating championships have been held over many years. It was on this Fen that the game 'Bandy' was invented; Bandy was the forerunner of ice hockey.

Above the Fen between the two villages there is a small path leading up to the site of an old windmill. According to legend a young girl cut her throat there and lay dying in a large pool of gore. Ever since, dressed in white, she has haunted this place, and at midnight every night, she can be seen walking along the small footpath to the mill. One night a man walking along this path to the mill saw something approaching him with a rattling sound and which was jolting along the path. It was a coffin being wheeled along the path. When the man saw it, he thought it was a friend playing a trick. However on shouting to his friend, the coffin lid rose and he saw a sight he would not disclose. There was a horrible chasm around the coffin, and suddenly in a flame of blue fire and with a terrible sound, like artillery fire, both coffin and bier vanished. The man then fainted. In the morning when he woke up, he returned home, dirty and dishevelled. He was greeted by his wife, who said he had been drunk and as such had fallen. Timid young men are told not to stay out late courting at this spot (in Tebbutt).

As defined by Vermuyden, the South Level lies to the south east of the Old Bedford River and the River Great Ouse.

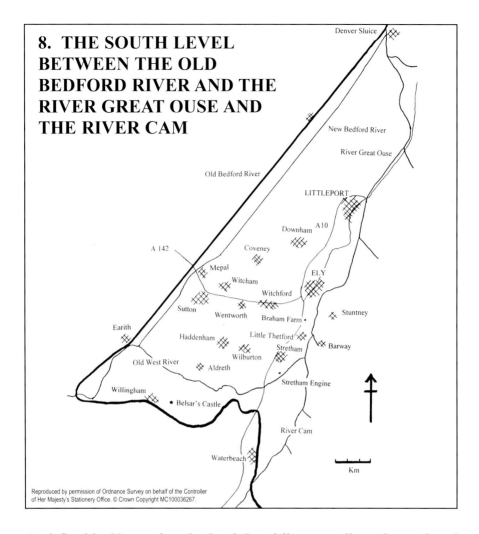

8. THE SOUTH LEVEL BETWEEN THE OLD BEDFORD RIVER AND THE RIVER GREAT OUSE AND THE RIVER CAM

Reproduced by permission of Ordnance Survey on behalf of the Controller of Her Majesty's Stationery Office. © Crown Copyright MC100036267.

As defined by Vermuyden, the South Level lies generally to the south and east of the Old Bedford River and parts of the River Great Ouse. On its northern, eastern and southern edges it is naturally bounded by rising ground in Norfolk, Suffolk and Cambridgeshire. The River Cam and that part of the River Great Ouse that flows past Ely, which flow in a generally northern direction, conveniently divide this level into two roughly equal areas.

Over lies in the south-western corner of that part of this level which lies between the Old Bedford River and the Rivers Great Ouse and Cam. Over means 'river bank' and the manor this village on the edge of Fenland village was given to Ramsey Abbey by Eadnoth II Bishop of Dorchester (1034–49). The chancel stalls of the church of St Mary are said to have come from that Abbey and the stone seats around the walls bring to mind the saying 'the weakest to the wall'.

75

The winter of 1947 had been very severe with deep snow. A thaw accompanied with heavy rain started on 10 March and on 13 March the rivers started to rise. During a night of gales on 16/17 March, waves 'broke over the top of the bank like the waves of the sea breaking across the quay of some fishing port' (Harvest Home, in Summers). Before long the Barrier Bank at Over Fen breached and it proved to be probably the most serious breach in Fenland. The waters soon covered the Fen and reached the landward side of the southern flood banks of the Old West River. These in turn breached and the flood waters poured right across Haddenham Fen towards Ely and the River Cam. Some 23,000ha of land were flooded, in places more than 2.5m deep in what was called 'possibly the greatest flood since the Fens were first drained'. This breach was finally sealed on 24 March by the army during their 'Operation Neptune' and which involved building a dam across the breach with old Neptune amphibious vehicles.

Some 5km to the east, between the two Fen edge villages of Willingham and Rampton, is Belsar's Hill and the Aldreth causeway. Belsar's Hill or Fort is now a simple oval earthwork. Its origins are not clear It possibly dates from the Iron Age. Alternatively, at the end of the 10th century, Willingham had been given to Ely and it could be that a castle was built or used to defend this outpost. Some say it was named after a Norman Commander, Belsar, who was seeking Hereward the Wake. The name 'Belleassise' was in use during the 13th century; this name may have been adopted earlier by Norman soldiers who had had to serve at this 'beautiful seat'. It may be the castle referred to as Aldreth Castle in King Stephen's reign, there being no record of any castle in Aldreth itself.

The fort lay on the ancient approach to the Isle of Ely from Cambridge; the Aldreth Causeway. Some say that the river crossing is the site of the Battle of Alrehede (Aldreth) between Hereward the Wake and William the Conqueror. Once again history becomes confused, but for a number of reasons it is unlikely that the bridge was the site of the battle. First the Ely Chronicles refer to a causeway being laid down here during the time of Bishop Hervey (1109–1131), i.e. after the supposed battle. This reference could however refer to some rebuilding. Secondly it is noteworthy and surprising that no artefacts consequent upon such a battle have been found here. Thirdly, to attack from such a position would have been strategically difficult as the site was overlooked from one of the highest spots on the Isle of Ely. Fourthly and most significantly, the geography does not correspond with contemporary accounts of the battle. So whilst the Normans almost certainly have set up camp at Belsar's Hill, they realised that they would not have much chance of success. Consequently they changed their direction of attack from Stuntney (see Chapter 9) to the Isle near Little Thetford.

Midway between Rampton and Cottenham, is the site of another, moated, fort. Its history too is uncertain and its construction appears to be incomplete. It may have been connected with the construction of the Car Dyke and the early Roman settlements near Cottenham. More plausibly, it may have been another of the forts built by King Stephen during his battles against Geoffrey de Mandeville. Part of the village was removed to make way for this unfinished fort and its abandonment may have been due to Geoffrey's defeat at Burwell Castle. To the north-east is Cottenham Lode and the Car Dyke. There are reports that William the Conqueror brought timber and stone to a quay here to be loaded onto boats and transported by river to strengthen Aldreth Causeway.

Denny Abbey (see Chapter 2) and Waterbeach are in the south-eastern corner of this part of the South Level. It was here that Charles Haddon Spurgeon (1834–1892) became the pastor of a little thatched chapel between 1852 and 1854. Known for baptising people in the nearby rivers, he became one of the most popular preachers in England. In 1854 he moved to London and preached at the Metropolitan Tabernacle which held some 6,000 persons; his sermons were published in weekly periodicals.

In complete contrast Marlowe tells of a witch who lived in a Fenland village close to the River Cam on the Car Dyke, quire probably Waterbeach. In 1835, an orphan, Rose Tooley, who had been strictly brought up by her aunt, fell in love and married her cousin Thomas Smith. For a number of years all was well, however a series of events was to disturb the village. First no wagon would pass their house, unless she or her husband appeared. Despite being whipped and beaten, the horses just reared and plunged; they would not move forward. However as soon as Rose or Thomas appeared, they immediately became docile and passed by with no problems.

Then some pigs 'were taken very queer, whirling round in the field and frothing at the mouth'. A man was called to slaughter them, but as soon as he appeared with his knife, they calmed down. A witch was stirring up trouble. Animals always stopped their actions when so threatened, lest the marks of a whip or knife would appear on the witch's body. Rose Smith was not yet suspected. This was soon to change. To prevent his cattle from further developing a plague, a local farmer resorted to an old charm. He caught a live toad and held it in a fire with tongs. With a loud explosion the toad vanished. The next day Rose appeared, looking as if her face, legs and thighs had been scorched and burnt, confirmation to all that she was the witch. After further similar events, the villagers nailed horse-shoes on their doors and placed crossed knives at every threshold to keep out Rose Smith.

Soon after, a group of workmen returning from their inn, saw a small black object floating above the hedge. As they watched, it transformed itself into Rose, who, now seated on a hurdle, flew off into the night. The men remained spell bound for an hour. Once safe at home, they decided to put Rose to the water test. Her husband protested, but that did no good and he was also accused. Wrapped in a sheet, with their toes and thumbs tied together, they were thrown into a pond. Here they floated and were thus 'rejected by the water, as they had rejected baptism through practising witchcraft'. Within a short time Rose died from exposure and fright. Now she was dead many came to see her laid out in her cottage. As they passed by, they were terrified by a loud squealing and howling which came from within a nearby chest of drawers. On opening it there was nothing inside and the villagers decided that the whole cottage and its contents should be destroyed. Whilst chest was being locked and the windows and doors being barred, the corpse was taken away for an uneventful burial. The cottage was set alight and when the fire was at its highest, there was a terrifying scream from Rose's room and a small black animal was seen running backwards and forwards. As the fire became fiercer, the object disappeared. The Devil had been burnt. As for Thomas, he escaped and fled to another village where he settled for the rest of his life. Although he was not considered to be a witch, he was not liked.

Stretham lies on the Roman Road between Cambridge and Ely. Submerged for much of the time between the 4th century and 17th century, a group of farmers and landowners set up a Drainage Commission to employ labourers to look after the drains, rivers and pumps. The first, the

Haddenham Level Commission, was established by parliament in 1727 to drain the Fens of Haddenham, Wilburton, and parts of Sutton and Stretham. To the south of the village is Stretham Engine. Built in 1831 by the Waterbeach Drainage Commission, to drain 2,500ha of Fenland, it replaced four windmills. The original steam engine was a 60hp Boulton and Watt steam double-acting rotating-beam engine which consumed five tonnes of coal a day. Initially it drove an 8.8m diameter scoop wheel which, as the Fen shrank had to be successively replaced. In 1850 the diameter was increased to 10m. By 1896 the engine's output was increased to 106hp to drive an 11.25m diameter scoop wheel with 48 scoops at 4rpm, lifting 30 tonnes of water per revolution. That wheel is now ineffective. The steam engine, preserved and replaced by diesel in 1925 and electric in 1943, was still operable in the early 1940s.

Between Stretham and Ely are Little Thetford and the medieval earthworks at Braham Farm. 'Thiutford' c972 and 'Liteltedford' c1086 both imply that here was a major river crossing. Possibly dating from the Bronze Age there was a crossing to Fordy and Barway on the east side of the Ouse. The earthworks at Braham Farm on the west bank of the River Great Ouse are most likely to have been associated with William the Conqueror's landing point on the Isle, having crossed from Stuntney. Such a crossing would have been the shortest route to the Isle, which matches contemporary measurements. Additionally a significant number of 11th century weapons have been recovered from the river here, in the early 14th century nearby land was called 'Herewardsbech', the local stream was called The Alderbrook and an area of land between Ely and Witchford is still called Alderforth. All this evidence suggests that the Battle of Alrehede was fought here and not at Aldreth.

The road from Stretham back to Earith runs along the southern high edge of the Isle of Ely, through Wilburton and Haddenham. Wilburton with the remains of ancient oaks, one of which is more than 6m round, was probably once on the edge a forest. It is an old village and two Bronze Age torcs, headbands of looped and twisted gold, were found in a nearby Fen, one in 1844 and the other in 1849 together with a gold bracelet and gold ring money. The Burystead is a splendid Elizabethan Manor House and an attractive group of houses near the church of St Peter recall the Dutch influence. A former rector, Thomas Alcock, later Bishop Alcock (1486–1500) entertained Henry VII here and a number of carved cocks in the church symbolise his residence.

Once forming three separate settlements, Haddenham, occupies one of the highest parts of the Isle of Ely, some 35m above sea level. Lying on the ancient road from Willingham, and Aldreth, it had the oldest church on the Isle, founded by St Ovin (Owine) in c. 673. When St Etheldreda's first husband died c655, Ovin administered her dowry. In c660 she became Queen of Northumbria and she took Ovin with her. Although he was not a scholar, he became a monk. It appears that when she returned to Ely in 673 to found her Abbey, he came south with her and may indeed have lived at Haddenham, the village which once had Ovin's Stone. Used for many years as a horse mounting block, it was the base of his cross which now stands beside the Prior's Door at Ely Cathedral. The stone is also in the Cathedral, having been taken there by James Bentham (1708–1794). The Latin inscription reads 'O God grant Thy light and rest to Ovin. Amen'. There is no trace of Ovin's church, although the Church of Holy Trinity, dating from the 13th century may stand on its site.

The Fen intrudes between Haddenham and Sutton to the north. Sutton's crowning glory is the beautiful tower of its church of St Andrew. The church and tower were built by Bishop Barnet (1366–1373) and his successor Bishop Thomas Arundel (1374–1388). Thomas became Bishop of Ely aged only 21. After Ely he went on to become Richard II's Chancellor and moved to York in 1388 from whence he crowned and assisted Henry VI. Hence the carvings in the south porch of the coats of arms of the two Bishops and of York, also the heads of a Bishop and a King, namely Bishop Arundel and Richard II. The tower was the latest work to be done on the church and it could be assumed that the inclusion of the coats of arms of York date it to be a little after 1388. The tower, the design of which was inspired by the Ely octagon tower, turns into a sturdy octagon supporting a taller and less bulky octagon with battlements and pinnacles. It is said that on a clear day, 40 other churches can be seen.

There is a story (in Mee) that a small stone bowl was found being used as a chicken feeding trough. That bowl, now in the church, is believed to have been the christening bowl from the nearby Burystead Monastery. There, there is an early 14th century chapel, originally two storeys, similar to Prior Crauden's Chapel in Ely. Nearby are the remains of a moat and fish ponds.

(See colour section for larger photo)

81

The only curve in the otherwise straight New Bedford River is around a small outlyer of the Isle of Ely which encompasses the village of Mepal. In the small church of St Mary, much restored but dating from the 13th century, is a tablet to James Fortrey, a refugee from Brabant. Amongst other things he was a page to the Duchess of York under Charles II and a groom to her husband James II.

During the Civil War when the Isle was held by Parliament, General Ireton built his road from Mepal across the Fen to Chatteris. Moving back onto the Isle, the five villages of Witcham, Wentworth, Witchford, Coveney, and Wardy Hill lie on a 4km diameter circle. Whilst the names of some of these might be considered to have some sinister connotations, there are none. Witcham takes its name from the 'wych elms' that once grew there. Wentworth is believed to be a corruption of Ovinsworth as St Ovine held land there. Witchford was where a north flowing river was forded by the early medieval road from Cambridge to Ely through Willingham, Aldreth, and Haddenham. Coveney was an 'ey' or island in the 'cove' or bay.

The largest of these villages, Witchford, held one of the two administrative courts on the medieval Isle of Ely and which met on the third Tuesday of each month. At an earlier date, it was at Witchford that the monks of Ely made their peace with William the Conqueror. It is said that he came unawares to their Abbey and whilst the monks were feeding, left a mark of gold on the altar. On learning of this visit, the monks went to the King to apologise, but at a price.

According to the *Liber Eliensis:*

'Afterwards, as the King was leaving, the said Gilbert de Kay came in to see the monastery, and after looking everywhere, found the monks at dinner in the refectory. "Oh wretched and foolish men," he said, "to sit here stuffing yourselves at this of all times, when the King is here and in your church." And there-upon they forsook the tables and rushed to the church, but could not find the King. Much perturbed, and having little hope save in God's providence, they besought Gilbert to intercede for them with the King lest ill befall. This he agreed to do and was able with some difficulty to obtain them an audience with a view to averting the royal wrath by prayers or presents. And being brought before the King at Witchford, where he then was, through the mediation of Gilbert and other nobles, they were received back in favour at the price of 700 marks of silver'. (in Manning).

Such was the severity of the fine, that they had to melt down church ornaments to pay it. When it was weighed, it was found to be deficient in weight and the monks were fined a further 300 marks. [It is difficult to assess the present day value of 1000 marks of silver. In 1910, Conneybeare calculated the value to be £20,000; at February 2002 this equates to about £1m].

It was to Coveney that the Saxon Noblewoman Aethelswyth retired with her maids to work at weaving and embroidery. She was the grand-daughter of Earldorman Byrhtnoth, and it was he who, on 10 August 991, 'came to meet them [the Danes at Maldon] with his levies and fought them, but they slew the Earldorman there and had possession of the place of slaughter. Afterwards peace was made with them'. (in Garmondsway). Her father and brother had been killed on 18 May 1010 when men from Cambridgeshire stood in vain against the Danes at the Battle of Hringmare Heath near Ringmere in Norfolk.

From its first occupation during the Iron Age, Little Downham was to become the home to the most favourite country palaces of the Bishops of Ely. Built by Bishop Alcock, it is said that five Bishops lived and died there. Probably its last occupant was Bishop Matthew Wren (1585–1667) who was arrested here in 1642. He had become Bishop of Ely in 1638 and had worked closely with William Laud (1573–1645), Archbishop of Canterbury, who was impeached of high treason in 1640, and condemned and beheaded in 1645. After Archbishop Laud's impeachment, Bishop Wren was arrested as a known supporter of Laud and imprisoned in the Tower of London from 1642 to 1660. At the restoration he was released and he returned to his See at Ely. After Wren's long imprisonment it is said (in Mee) that on being warned of his conduct by Charles II, he replied in a moment of boldness that he knew his way to the Tower.

Moving off the Isle of Ely towards the New Bedford River is a hamlet of Little Downham, Pymore. A nearby pumping station records drainage developments from the 18th century windmills to the coming of steam in 1830.

> *'These Fens have oft times been by* Water *drown'd.*
> *Science a remedy in* Water *found.*
> *The powers of* Steam *she said shall be employ'd*
> *and the* Destroyer *by Itself destroyed.*

(In Darby)

To the north of Ely, Littleport is somewhat of an enigma. It is difficult to understand why, situated on an island, it did not assume a greater importance. Perhaps it was always overshadowed by Ely. Certainly it is in a lonely part of the country; 'the loneliest spot within 100 miles of London' where 'it was as rare to see a coach in Littleport as a ship in Newmarket'.

This loneliness and the associated poverty, starvation and exploitation was the background to the Littleport Riots of 1816. The local labourers had been provoked once to often by the landowners. They rebelled and gathered at the Globe Public House awaiting other followers from Southery and Denver, before marching to the Vicarage to confront the Rev Vachell, vicar and magistrate. Whilst he agreed to try to meet some of their demands, it was not enough for the rioters. Despite being read the Riot Act by the vicar, they went on a drunken rampage attacking a number of houses including the Vicarage. The vicar and his family fled for safety to Ely where they sought help.

In their turn the rioters also marched to Ely, now armed with an assortment of weapons including pistols and a wagon carrying a large Fenland punt gun. Once again their demands were met by the magistrates and they were all pardoned for their riotous behaviour. Whilst some returned to Littleport, others continued their rampage through-out Ely before they too returned to Littleport. However the Home Secretary's help had already been sought and the rebellion was ruthlessly put down by the dragoons and yeomanry of Sir Henry Bate Dudley, 'The Fighting Parson'. One rioter was killed and 98 arrested. Of those arrested, 76 were tried by Edward Christian, brother of Fletcher Christian of the Bounty. On 22 June, 24 were sentenced to death, although later 19 had their sentences commuted to imprisonment or transportation. The remaining five were executed on 28 June. As one rioter had remarked earlier 'I might as well be hanged as be starved'.

These lonely Fens stretch north to Denver passing Apes hall, formerly Apseholte, first recorded in 1251 where some 30ha of land had been reclaimed. Ely, from the Saxon Elig or Latin Elge meaning Eel Island, however dominates all the Fens of the South Level. The small city clusters round its great cathedral and former monastic buildings. Dating from 1081, it is the third longest church in England; 164m. On the floor below the west tower is a maze, which if straightened out will equal the height of the tower; 66m. Perhaps one of the finest features is the Octagon Tower.

When the early Norman tower collapsed Alan of Walsingham planned in 1322 an eight sided tower as its replacement. There were to be eight large piers forming an irregular octagon with four short and four long sides. A wooden vaulted roof covering a span of 22.5m was to support a smaller octagonal Lantern Tower. The corner posts are made of great oak pillars, 19m long and nearly 1.25m in diameter. They are said to have come by river from a great forest near Chicksands in Bedfordshire. Its top is over 43m above the aisle.

The Cathedral suffered under Oliver Cromwell. Despite being the Governor of the Isle Of Ely, Champion of the Rights of Fenmen, and living in the City, he decapitated all but one of the delicate statues in the Lady Chapel. In January 1644, he closed it for 17 years. His home for a while was Cromwell House, which dates from the 13th century. Allegedly haunted, it has been used as the vicarage for the nearby church of Holy Trinity and St Mary, and a pub. The cannon on the Green, given to the City after its capture from the Russians at Sebastopol, is aimed almost directly at this house.

The Cathedral is surrounded by associated buildings. To the south-west is Bishop Alcock's principal 15th century Palace, in whose garden is one of the largest and oldest Plane Trees in the country. To the south are two groups of houses. First in a Norman arcade are the remains of the 12th century Infirmary, including Powcher's Hall (after William Powcher, Prior in 1401), which was used as the blood-letting house where Monks were bled by leaches to keep their bodies clean. Secondly close to the site of the Refectory and Monk's kitchen are the Guest Hall and the Prior's Hall. This latter Hall stands next to the two storey Crauden's Chapel, built by Alan of Walsingham for Prior (later Bishop) John Crauden in 1324.

Further to the south is the 14th century Ely Porta, one of the entrances to the Cathedral, but also used as the Manor Court and, on occasions, as a prison. The Park leads past the remains of a motte and bailey castle used to protect Ely from attacks launched from the 'mainland' at Stuntney. The monks built a windmill here to grind the flour stored in the nearby medieval granary. At the bottom of the hill is the River Great Ouse, across which lies the remainder of the South Level.

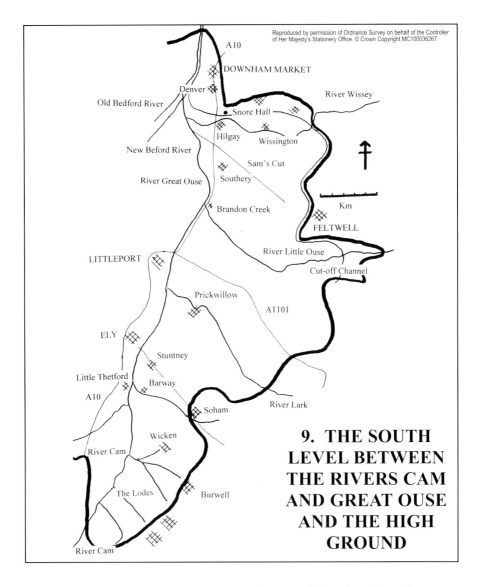

A10

DOWNHAM MARKET

Denver

River Wissey

Old Bedford River

Snore Hall

Hilgay

Wissington

New Beford River

Sam's Cut

River Great Ouse   Southery

Km

Brandon Creek

FELTWELL

LITTLEPORT

River Little Ouse

Cut-off Channel

Prickwillow

A1101

ELY

Stuntney

Little Thetford

Barway

A10

Soham

River Lark

Wicken

9. THE SOUTH LEVEL BETWEEN THE RIVERS CAM AND GREAT OUSE AND THE HIGH GROUND

River Cam

The Lodes   Burwell

River Cam

The islands of Stuntney and Barway, to the east of the River Great Ouse, are two 'stepping stones' to the higher land at Soham. The isle of Stuntney, 'steep', rises abruptly from the Fens, perhaps consequent on the ancient River Cam which originally flowed close by and not through Ely. Its course, at the foot of the isle is marked by roddons which here show up as light coloured bands against the darker fen soils. According to legend, the route of the causeway from Ely to Soham via Stuntney, was revealed to St Edmund in a dream, when he wished to visit St Etheldreda. It is likely however that there had been a causeway here for centuries; a Bronze Age hoard was found here in 1939 as well as Roman artefacts and indeed it became a Roman road connecting Ely with Colchester. Also used by the monks it became a well used crossing between St Etheldreda's monastery in Ely and St Felix' monastery in Soham.

Stuntney, Calcetum de Stuntney, with its substantially rebuilt Norman church of St Cross, was both a chapelry and a prosperous grange of Ely. It had one of the most important fisheries in Cambridgeshire; the annual gift of eels in 1086 was 24,000. A new wooden bridge was built on the causeway between 1339–1340. In 1832 the bridge was still made of timber, but had to be rebuilt with stone arches because the old structure hindered navigation. In 1908, that was replaced by a single span bridge.

The Tudor Stuntney Old Hall was the home of the Stewards. Elizabeth Steward, daughter of William Steward, collector of the Ely tithes, was Oliver Cromwell's mother. Her brother, Prior Robert of Wells or Steward became the last Prior and first Dean of Ely in 1522, a post which he held until the Dissolution in 1539. Perhaps somewhat ironically Oliver Cromwell was to inherit the Hall from his uncle.

Celia Fiennes, travelling between Bury St Edmunds and Newmarket in 1698, made a detour to Ely via the causeway at Stuntney. It crossed 'low moorish ground' where peat was cut. She had the general impression of an 'unhealthy countryside, frequently flooded, divided by "deep ditches with draines" and inhabited by "a lazy sort of people" occupied in repairing banks and in the breeding and grasseing of cattle'. (in Darby).

The second of the stepping stones was to the small island of Barway, meaning 'Bird Island', on the edge of the former Soham Mere. In the 1930s, excavations revealed the remains of a late Bronze Age causeway crossing the River Cam from Old Fordey Farm towards Little Thetford. The straight causeway was found to be about 6m wide and built with 2.5m piles every 1m, supporting a mat of boughs and faggots which in turn carried a layer of sand and gravel. It seems most likely that William the Conqueror travelled from his camp at Weeting through Wicken, Padney, and Old Fordey, to Little Thetford. Not only have 11th century weapons and other artefacts associated with a major battle been found here, but the distances between Stuntney and Barway and Little Thetford and Braham Farm are more consistent with those quoted in *Gestis Herwardi* than those between Willingham and Aldreth.

Besides the causeway, there was another means by which Soham could be reached, namely by Soham Lode, the largest of the Cambridgeshire Roman Lodes, Lode being a medieval word for waterway. Some say they were built as boundary markers or extensions of upland defences. It is more likely however that these unique waterways were built by the Romans primarily for transport from the Rivers Great Ouse and Cam, across the Fens to the Fenland and Fen edge villages of Soham, Wicken, Burwell, Reach,

Swaffham Bulbeck, Commercial End, Swaffham Prior, Lode, Stow cum Quy and Bottisham. Not only did they serve as navigation channels, but they carried water from the chalk uplands across the Fens, which they also drained. They were extensively used commercially during the 17th century and 18th century, however with the coming of the railways in 1884, this use declined rapidly.

As the Fens were drained, the consequent shrinkage caused a problem for the future maintenance of the Lodes. Should they be preserved as 'high level' carriers or should they be made redundant by a series of new 'low level' carriers? After much debate they have been preserved as 'high level' embanked, generally navigable, waterways.

Although, with the exception of Wicken, the villages at the ends of the Lodes lie strictly outside the confines of the South Level as defined, they have a relevance to the Fens. Soham lay on the edge of Soham Mere (c650ha), a significant fishery at Doomsday. Whilst some reclamation started in 1594, it was finally drained in the second half of the 18th century. Although a steam pump had been recommended in 1789, it was to be 50 years before one was built. Indeed a windmill was still in use 150 years later. At Burwell, meaning 'Spring by the Fort', King Stephen started building a castle on the site of a Roman fortification. It was here, whilst the fort was being built, that it was attacked by the rebel Geoffrey de Mandeville, who was killed in the ensuing battle. The castle was never finished and the site was later used as a manor of the Ramsey abbots.

Reach lies at the end of the Devil's Ditch and Reach Lode appears as an extension across the Fens to the River Cam. Long ago, when there was a forest here, there was a chief Hrothgar whose daughter Hayenna was desired by the Fire Demon. Hrothgar told her not to worry as his god was the Water God, sworn enemy to the Fire Demon. One night Hrothgar had a dream in which an old man told him to prepare for a battle against the Fire Demon and his new ally the Tempest God. The old man promised to help Hrothgar and told him what should be done. The next day he outlined his plans to all the giants of the forest. First they cut down all the trees to give a long wide clearing. During the next three days they built a trench from the river to Mount Dithon, 18ft deep and seven miles long. The Tempest God had watched their work and sent a strong east wind to blow down the forest on top of them. The storm also brought rain, hail and snow. The giants rounded on Hrothgar saying that he had angered the gods and he should not have crossed the Fire Demon. As he was telling them not to be afraid because the Water God would protect them, the rain ceased. Under a great cloud of smoke, a huge wall of fire rushed towards the trench. All but Hrothgar fled. However he came out from his hiding and with his bare hands dug away the strip of earth separating the river from the trench. The water poured into the trench with a mighty roar. The Fire Demon was powerless against this broad channel of water and the fire died down, the tempest abated and Hayenna was safe. The ditch, the Devil's Dyke extending to Wood Ditton (Mount Dithon), is still there. So is its extension, Reach Lode. (in Marlowe).

The village developed rapidly from its Iron Age origins, into a major early medieval trading station with docks for sea going ships. Such was its importance that tradition said that when Cambridge was but a village, Reach was a city with nine churches. Between Swaffham Bulbeck and Swaffham Prior, famous for its two churches, St Mary and St Cyriac, sharing the same church yard, is Commercial End. Like Reach it too was an inland port catering for sea going vessels. Close by the docks would have been the small Benedictine Priory for nuns founded by the Bolbecs and of which there are a few remains. Bottisham Lode leads to Lode, Bottisham, and to Quy at the extreme south eastern limit of the Fens.

(See colour section for larger photo)

As its name implies, Wicken Lode leads to Wicken Fen and Wicken village. Formerly Wigingamere, meaning Dairy Farms, Wicken was granted a three day fair of St Laurence in 1331. One of Oliver Cromwell's sons, Henry Cromwell, Governor General of Ireland, lived at Spinney Abbey nearby and is buried in the parish church of St Laurence. White poppies can still be seen growing in the village, and up to the end of the 19th century, tea made from their heads was considered to be the only effective remedy against ague. Other, arguably stranger cures or palliatives were practised here. In one family, the wife applied hot pancakes to her body to relieve her back pain, whilst in hot weather her husband put fresh grass in his boots to keep his feet cool. In the village there is a restored smock mill, whilst in Wicken Fen is another smock mill; not one which grinds corn but which pumped water.

Before the coming of steam driven drainage pumps, wind pumps were a very common feature of the Fens. Just before the introduction of steam, a survey undertaken in 1821 showed there were 75 wind driven pumps in the South Level. Whilst to all intents and purposes they were like corn mills, the drive turned a large wooden wheel with paddles, scoops, or ladles which scooped or lifted the water up into the higher drains. The windmill at Wicken Fen was moved from Adventurers Fen in 1908 and re-assembled at Wicken. It is however hardly a typical wind-pump. It was actually used to lift water from the surrounding low lying Fen up into the artificially maintained Wicken Fen. In other words it was working backwards. By 1888 steam had taken over; only six wind-pumps survived and the remainder had been replaced by 32 steam driven pumps.

Wicken Fen itself, a naturalists' paradise, rich in plants, insects, and birds, is an artificially maintained and managed peat and sedge wetland presently covering some 300ha (more is planned). Whilst it is neither a 'real' Fen, as it stands some 2m or more above the surrounding land, nor is it truly a relic of an ancient Fenland, it must reflect Fenland as it was. Certainly it has its own unique atmosphere, best expressed by Wentworth Day (in Scarfe).

The scent of reeds and peaty waters,
of sallows and meadowsweet,
of rotten lily pads – and of fish:
It belonged to an untamed, undrained England.

In the early 19th century, a certain Joseph Hempsall lived near Soham. He was accustomed to walking across the Fens, through Wicken to Upware and to its inn, 'Five Miles from Anywhere – No Hurry', formerly the Lord Nelson. He knew the pit-falls and the treacherous Big Bog. One evening near Christmas whilst he was drinking at the inn, a dense fog suddenly descended; so dense that it was impossible to see more than a yard ahead. Despite the efforts of his friends to dissuade him, he set off home on his usual route across the Fen.

The fog lasted three days and nothing was heard of Joseph. On the fourth day it eventually cleared and a friend, Elijah Boggers, set off to visit Joseph at his farm. On his way he saw Joseph coming towards him, but he did not seem to be quite the jovial, blustering Fenlander they all knew. Without saying a word Joseph turned around and walked back towards his farm with Elijah. Within earshot of the farm Joseph suddenly said 'in a hollow sepulchral tone "go not in there – my body lies in Big Bog" '.

Before the terrified Elijah could reply, Joseph put a freezing hand on his shoulder and continued speaking. "As I am now, so one day wilt thou be. I lost my life in Big Bog on the first night of the fog – go to Eaudyke and there wilt thou find my body." Although he was petrified, Elijah did as he was asked and found Joseph's body lying half in and half out of the water of Big Bog, covered with mud and slime.

Elijah fled for his life back to the inn where, when he had recovered from his shock, he told his story. With a group of other friends, he returned to the spot where he had found the body, but search as they would, they could not find it; it had disappeared. As they were about to leave, Joseph suddenly appeared beside them saying "Fear not – as I am now so must ye all be – recover my body from the west side of Big Bog and bury it in Wicken churchyard."

A short time after the friends found Joseph's body as he had said. However they did not take it to Wicken; they took it to Soham where it was buried. His ghost haunts the Fens and on foggy nights cries and groans of

Joseph's dying agonies are heard 'ere the waters of the dyke closed his earthly mouth for ever'. Joseph's ghost will not rest until he is buried in Wicken churchyard. (in Marlowe).

Upware, a short distance from Wicken has been both a Republic and a Kingdom. In 1851 a group of Cambridge undergraduates formed a sporting club, known as The Upware Republic. To escape from the academic life, they chose this place to enjoy fishing and boating in the summer and skating in the winter. Under its constitution, it printed its own money and passed its own laws. The officials included, a Consul, a President, a State Chaplain, a Professor, a Champion, a Minister of Education, an Interpreter, a Tapster, a Treasurer, and a Secretary. The landlord of the inn was the Vice-consul and a local Irish labourer became the State Fiddler.

Amongst the hundreds of members of and visitors to the Republic were, the mathematician Joseph Wolstenholme, John Grant, later Sir John, Solicitor-General and Under-Secretary for India, Archibald Lewin Smith, later Sir Archibald, Master of the Rolls and Henry Morgan later master of Jesus College, Cambridge.

In 1866 the Republic ceased to exist. However 10 years later a Cambridge eccentric, Richard Ramsey Fielder of Jesus College, proclaimed himself King of Upware. Dressed in a scarlet waistcoat with corduroy breeches, he spent much of his time drinking and quarrelling with the passing bargees. Although they were a very tough breed, he was a match for most of them. He kept with him an enormous brown earthenware jug which held at least 23 litres (6 gallons) of punch. Made specially for him and decorated with his initials and crest, it was known as 'His Majesty's Pint'. With the coming of the railways, river traffic, and the number of bargees, declined. He 'forswore sack and lived cleanly' (in Wentworth Day) retiring to live in respectability in Folkestone.

The South Level boundary crosses the River Cam near Clayhithe, where a ferry existed from the early 14th century to the 1870s, towards Stow cum Quy in the extreme south-east corner of the Level. Accessible by river from Bottisham Lode and Quy Water, considerable river trade took place at the weather boarded Lode Mill and at Quy where remains of moorings can be found in farm walls.

Originally two villages, Stow with its church of St Mary is on the high ground. Quy, a corruption of 'Cow Island' on the edge of the Fens had its church in the Middle Ages. In 1650 Jeremy Collier (1650–1726) was born at Quy. He was educated in Ipswich and at Caius College in Cambridge. He became a very high churchman, almost Roman Catholic in his beliefs. He supported James II and refused allegiance to William II whom he railed against in sermons and in pamphlets. After accompanying two men, who had plotted to assassinate the King, to their execution, he publicly absolved them of their crimes from the scaffold. Outlawed in 1696, he was ordained a nonjuring Bishop in 1713. He attacked all forms of profanity on the stage and thus opened the door to decent comedy and drama.

North of the causeway between Ely and Stuntney there is an association with another, later, William; William IV. A local pub was named after his unpopular wife, Queen Adelaide. Although the pub is no longer there, her name lives on in the small settlement of Queen Adelaide and in the Adelaide course on the River Great Ouse, where the Cambridge University boat race crews train for the annual Oxford Cambridge boat race.

To the east, Prickwillow, derived from the 'pricks' or skewers made from local willow, lies on the ancient roddons of the Rivers Great Ouse and Lark. The parish church of St Peter, built on piles in 1868, contains a white 17th century Italian marble font, originally from Ely Cathedral. The consequences of Fen drainage are all too evident here. When the vicarage was first built, presumably with its foundations in the underlying clay, the front door had two steps. Now there are nine and former cellars are ground floor rooms. Another consequence is that any attempt to dig a grave here would simply result in a hole full of water.

Fittingly Prickwillow has a Drainage Engine Museum. This houses engines such as a Vickers Petter two-cylinder, a three-cylinder Allen, single-cylinder Ruston and Lister engines and a five-cylinder Mirrlees Beckerton and Day diesel engine dating from 1923. This latter engine was capable of lifting 140 tonnes of water per minute and although it was replaced by a modern diesel engine in 1974, it remained on standby duty until 1981/2.

A strange tale is told of a lady who came from India to live near Prickwillow with her 'child'. This child was a wild one, appearing to be half human and half ape. She was captured and taken to Cambridge. However she escaped and ran home terrifying people all along the way. She was shot at and wounded as she made her way. She then started killing anyone who stood in her way. Once home she strangled her 'mother' and died soon after. On misty night at the old home two shadowy figures can be seen; one a lady, the other an ape with its hairy arm around the lady's waist.

Upstream from Prickwillow, the River Lark, flowing in an artificial, probably Roman, channel passes Isleham. Although the village itself lies outside the South Level, the river has been used since the mid-19th century for baptism by total immersion. The Rev Charles Haddon Spurgeon, 'The Prince of Preachers' was himself baptised here on 3 May 1850. The service was originally held in the open river channel, however when a new weir was built in a loop of the river, the service was held in the over-fall. The weir however caused the water to become sluggish and stagnant. In 1972, the Minister, the Rev Chipper, announced the end of the practice because those who had been baptised came out 'smelling rather'.

Between the River Lark and the River Little Ouse are some of the best examples of roddons in East Anglia. As they cross and re-cross the A1101, they show up as light coloured silt bands standing proud of the darker low lying Fenland peats. Like the River Lark, the River Little Ouse flows in an artificial channel, again probably Roman, between Brandon Creek and Botany Bay. Brandon Creek, on the border between Cambridgeshire and Norfolk was supposedly the site of macabre deaths for prisoners of war working for the Dutch engineers in the middle of the 17th century. Some, when the tide was out, were buried up to their necks in the muddy river banks. As the tide came in, so they slowly drowned. Others when the tide was in, were made to stand on barges with a noose around their necks tied to overhanging trees. As the tide dropped, so they were slowly strangled.

Continuing north, through Southery, Hilgay lies on the River Wissey. It is known for two very contrasting people. First was Phineas Fletcher (1582–1650) who was rector of Hilgay between 1621 and 1650. In an imitation of Spencer's Faery Queene, he wrote in 1633 'The Purple Island or the Isle of Man'. In a series of 12 works, he surveyed the vices and virtues of man in which he considered the body as an island, the bones as foundations and the veins as books and so on. The second, although a soldier trained to kill, was also concerned with life, namely George William Manby (1765–1854). Shocked by witnessing the wreck of a Government ship close to the shore with scores of men drowning before him, he developed a schoolboy idea of firing a rope to a ship. Having practised from the tower of Hilgay church, of which he was a church-warden, his device was successfully used in 1808 on the brig Elizabeth. Within 15 years 230 had been saved and for which he was rewarded by the Government in the sum of £2,000.

During the middle of his life, in 1809, a tale was told of a periodical visit every six or seven years to Hilgay Fen by a plague of field mice. They immediately began to devour everything in sight. The land would have been laid bare but for a great flight of white horned owls which arrived as if by instinct from Norway. They destroyed all the mice and then disappeared as suddenly as they had arrived. (in Harper).

Opposite Hilgay on the north bank of the River Wissey are Fordham and Snore (Snowre) Hall. Dating from the 15th century, the hall was owned by the Skipworth family, a Catholic family who installed a chapel in the roof and where Nicholas Owen built a double priest hole. Charles I is said to have stayed here on his journey from Oxford to Newark. It was here that he held his last council of war. Whether he went straight to Newark is not clear for there is an account that he stayed in Downham Market on May Day 1646, disguised as a clergyman. The 15th century brickwork on the west side of the house is one of the earliest examples of domestic brickwork in England.

In contrast to Snore Hall, a very odd house had been built at West Dereham. The central feature of this house, which stretched to five bays on either side, was the gate-house of the former West Dereham Abbey. This was a Premonstratensian house built by Hubert Walter in 1188; its fine gate-house had octagonal towers. At the Dissolution, the lands were given to Francis Dereham, whose friendship with Catherine Howard would, at the hands of Henry VIII, cost him his life. Sir Thomas Dereham, envoy to James II, incorporated the tower in his grand designs in 1697. During Georgian times the property deteriorated and now only the site remains.

To the north of Snore Hall, in the grounds of Ryston Hall is Kett's Oak. After Kett's Rebellion in 1549, it is said that some of the renegades were hung from this tree.

'Surely the tree that nine men did twist on
Must be the old oak tree now at Ryston'

(in Harper).

The turn-pike road to King's Lynn continues through Denver, birthplace of William Manby, and Downham Market, where Horatio Nelson and William Manby attended school, to leave the South Level near Wimbotsham. The River Great Ouse flows likewise towards King's Lynn, leaving the controls at Denver to flow freely under Stowbridge to the sea.

'Water with banks confin'd as in a Gaol
Till kinder Sluices let them go on Bail.
Samuel Fortrey (1685).

SOURCES, REFERENCES AND
FURTHER READING

The Author gratefully acknowledges the authors of the following publications which have been used extensively as sources and references whilst researching the background to this book.

A Dictionary of English Place Names, A. D. Mills, Oxford, 1991.

A Geology for Engineers, F. G. H. Blyth, Arnold, 1961.

A History of Huntingdonshire, M. Wickes, Oxford, 1985.

A Short History of Ely Cathedral, S. Evans, Camb. Univ. Press, 1946.

A View into Cambridgeshire, M. Rouse, Dalton, 1974.

Anglo Saxon England, P. Hunter Blair, Camb. Univ. Press. 1956.

Bedfordshire and Huntingdonshire, A. Mee, Hodder and Stoughton, 1973.

Call it a Summer Country, E. Storey, Hale, 1978.

Cambridgeshire, E. A. R. Ennion, Hale, 1951.

Cambridgeshire, A. Mee, Hodder and Stoughton, 1939.

Cambridgeshire, O. Cook, Blackie, 1953.

Cambridgeshire, N. Scarfe, Faber & Faber, 1983.

Cambridgeshire Customs and Folklore, E. Porter, Routledge, Kegan Paul, 1969.

Curiosities of Rural Cambridgeshire, P. Jeever, Oleander Press, 1977.

East Anglia, H. Meredith, Robert Scott,

East Anglia, R. H. Mottram, Chapman and Hall, 1933.

East Anglia, H. Innes, Hodder and Stoughton, 1990.

East Anglia, P Steggall, Hale, 1979.

East Anglia, D. Wallace, Batsford, 1939.

East Anglian Album, I. C. Allen, Oxford Publishing Co., 1976.

Ely Town Trail and Mini Guide to Ely, East Cambs. Dist. Council, 1999.

England's Thousand Best Churches, S. Jenkins, Penguin, 1999.

Fenland; Its Ancient Past and Uncertain Future, H. Godwin, Camb. Univ. Press, 1978.

Fenland River, R. Tibbs, Dalton, 1969.

Fenland Rivers, I. Wedgewood, Rich and Cowan, 1936.

Fenland Waterways, M. Roulstone, Balfour, 1974.

Flag Fen, www.eastmidlands.info/flagfen, J. Byford, 2003.

Forgotten Railways of East Anglia, R. S. Joby, David and Charles, 1977.

Geology and Scenery in England and Wales. A. E. Trueman, Pelican, 1963.

Ghosts and Legends of Lincolnshire and the Fen Country, P. Howat, Countryside Books, 1992.

Great Ouse Country, A. Hunter Blair, John Nickalls Publications, 2002.

Highways and Byways in Cambridge and Ely, E. Conybeare, Macmillan, 1910.

Highways and Byways in East Anglia, W. Dutt, Macmillan, 1901.

Historical Memorials of Ely Cathedral. C. W. Stubbs, Dent, 1897.

History of Bluntisham cum Earith, C. F. Tebbutt, 1941.

History of the Fens, J. Wentworth-Day, S.R. Publishers, 1970.

Inland Waterways of Great Britain, J. Cumberlidge, Imray, 1998.

Legends of the Fenland People, C. Marlowe, Palmer, 1926.

Liable to Floods, J. R. Ravensdale, Camb. Univ. Press, 1974.

Lincolnshire, H. Thorold & J Yates, Faber & Faber, 1965.

Lord Orford's Voyage Around the fens, Intr. H. J. K. Jenkins, Cambs. Library Publs, 1987.

Norfolk, B. Dorman, Batsford, 1972.

Norfolk, A. Mee, Hodder and Stoughton, 1940.

Norfolk, W. Harrod and C. L. S. Linnell, Faber, 1969.

Norfolk, W. Harrod, Faber, 1982.

Norfolk Villages, D. H. Kennett, Hale, 1980.

Portrait of Cambridgeshire, S. A. Manning, Hale, 1978.

Portrait of the Fen Country, E. Storey, Hale, 1972.

Portrait of Norfolk, D. Yaxley, Hale, 1977.

Rivers, R. Russell, David and Charles, 1978.

Rivers of East Anglia, J. Turner, Cassell, 1954.

Roman Britain and Early England, P. Hunter Blair, Sphere Books, 1975.

Suffolk and Norfolk, M. R. James, Dent, 1930.

The Anglo Saxon Chronicles, Trl. G. N. Garmonsway, Dent, 1953.

The Black Fens, A. K. Astbury, EP Publishing, 1973.

The Buildings of Bedfordshire, and the County of Huntingdon and Peterborough, N. Pevsner, Penguin Books, 1974.

The Buildings of England, Cambridgeshire, N. Pevsner, Penguin, 1954.

The Buildings of England, North West and South Norfolk, N. Pevsner, Penguin, 1962.

The Cambridge, Ely and King's Lynn Road, C. G. Harper, Chapman and Hall, 1902.

The Cambridgeshire Landscape, C. Taylor, Hodder and Stoughton, 1973.

The Changing Fenland, H. C. Darby, Camb. Univ. Press, 1983.

The Concise Dictionary of National Biography, Oxford, 1992.

The Concise Oxford Dictionary of English Place Names, E. Ekwall, Oxford, 1976.

The Draining of the Fens, H. C. Darby, Camb. Univ. Press, 1940.

The Fenland Past and Present, S. H. Miller and S. B .J. Skertchley, Longmans, 1878.

The Fens, A. Bloom, Robert Hale, 1953.

The Great Level, D. Summers, David and Charles, 1976.

The Great Ouse, D. Summers, David and Charles, 1973.

The Medieval Fenland, H. C. Darby, David and Charles, 1974.

The Middle Level, A. Hunter Blair, Imray Laurie Norie and Wilson, 2000.

The Origins of Norfolk, T. Williamson, Manchester Univ. Press, 1993.

The Ouse, A. J. Foster, SPCK.

The River Great Ouse and Tributaries, A. Hunter Blair, Imray Laurie Norie and Wilson, 2000.

The Shell Guide to England, Ed. J. Hadfield, Michael Joseph, 1970.

The Skaters of the Fens, A. Bloom, Heffer, 1958.

Vermuyden and the Fens, L. E Harris, Cleaver Hume, 1953.

Currency conversions are based on the modern equivalent purchasing power, the data being kindly provided by the Public Enquiries Group of the Bank of England.

LOCAL TITLES
PUBLISHED BY JOHN NICKALLS
PUBLICATIONS

A GARLAND OF WAVENEY
VALLEY TALES
A compilation of illustrated tales from
Suffolk of yesteryear

A PHARMACIST'S TALE
The joys, delights and
disappointments encountered
preserving pharmacy history

CURIOUSITIES OF NORFOLK
A county guide to the unusual

GREAT OUSE COUNTRY
Sketches of its riverside folk and
history from source to mouth

MELTON CONSTABLE, BRISTON
& DISTRICT – BOOK ONE
A portrait in old picture postcards

MELTON CONSTABLE, BRISTON
& DISTRICT – BOOK TWO
A further portrait in old picture
postcards

NATURE TRAILS IN
NORTHAMPTONSHIRE

NEWMARKET, TOWN AND TURF
A pictorial tour

NORTH NORFOLK
A portrait in old picture postcards

NORWICH – THEN AND NOW
A look at the city through
old postcards and modern
photographs

IN AND AROUND NORWICH –
THEN AND NOW
A further look at Norwich
and district

NORWICH – THEN AND NOW
A third selection of old picture
postcards

ROBBER BARONS AND
FIGHTING BISHOPS
The Medieval Chronicles
of East Anglia

SHIRES, SALES AND PIGS
The story of an Ely family of
Auctioneers. George Comins,
1856–1997

SUFFOLK'S LIFEBOATS
A portrait in postcards and
photographs

S'WONDERFUL
A symphony of musical memories

'SMARVELLOUS
More musical memories